THEY SAID
I WAS LEAVING
AT EIGHT

THEY SAID I WAS LEAVING AT EIGHT

A Journey to Acceptance and
Letting Go of This Life.

CAROLE MCMECHAN/DAVIS

THEY SAID I WAS LEAVING AT EIGHT
A JOURNEY TO ACCEPTANCE AND LETTING GO OF THIS LIFE.

iUniverse books may be ordered through booksellers or by contacting:

iUniverse
1663 Liberty Drive
Bloomington, IN 47403
www.iuniverse.com
1-800-Authors (1-800-288-4677)

ISBN: 978-1-5320-4557-8 (sc)
ISBN: 978-1-5320-4562-2 (e)

Library of Congress Control Number: 2018903313

Print information available on the last page.

iUniverse rev. date: 05/02/2019

For my son Nigel and my daughter Tess.

Contents

Acknowledgments... ix

It's Just the Beginning xi

Chapter 1 1

Chapter 2 5

Chapter 3 18

Chapter 4 25

Chapter 5 35

Chapter 6 45

Chapter 7 50

Chapter 8 64

Chapter 9 78

Chapter 10 82

Chapter 11 88

Chapter 12 98

Chapter 13 103

Chapter 14 108

Chapter 15 127

Chapter 16 139

Chapter 17 148

Chapter 18 157

Chapter 19 164

Chapter 20 169

Chapter 21 180

Chapter 22 185

Chapter 23 192

Chapter 24 196

Chapter 25 212

Bibliography...219

About the Author 221

Acknowledgments

I would like to thank my children Tess and Nigel, and John, my husband, for their loving support throughout the process of completing this book. I would like to thank Corky and Grandpa Archie for being so supportive and loving and taking such good care of my mother in her time of need. To my brother Vern, thank you for all your love and support through this intense journey. I couldn't have done it without you. Thanks to my editor Susan Chambers for all her insights. I am gratefully indebted to you all.

It's Just the Beginning

It was a crisp winter morning, just before the hectic wind-up to Christmas. I sat alone at the kitchen table, savoring my first cup of coffee and a few moments of peace. My family was still asleep, and our dog, Kira, lay quietly at my feet. Opening the newly arrived morning paper, I was idly browsing through the various sections when my eye caught the heading, "Hospital Costs Critical." I wondered, critical to what and to whom?

I read on. A study on the elderly and terminally ill patients had recently been completed, and statistics were being compiled that compared the cost of hospital care versus home care nursing. I cannot explain why I stopped to read this article. At that time, I knew of no elderly or terminally ill people needing nursing care. Little did I know that my family and I would become part of those statistics before the following year had finished.

Chapter 1

Christmas was fast approaching, and I was busy wrapping presents, baking cookies, and decorating the house for the festivities ahead. The kids were counting down the days until Santa would arrive at our house.

It was Christmas Eve day, and I was running around town, getting the last odds and ends for the big day. I had just picked up the Christmas turkey and was putting it in the van when I met my mother in the parking lot of the grocery store.

I called out to her, "Mom! What a surprise! I was just going to call you to find out what time you're coming over tonight."

Mom said, "I thought I'd come around dinner time." She paused, "You know, I think I have the stomach flu—at least, that's what the doctor said. I was just going into the grocery store to buy some apple juice. If I drink only fluids today, my stomach should settle down."

"Oh, I'm so sorry you are sick. Why don't you come to our house and stay with us for a few days," I asked. "We'll take care of you, and it will be so nice to have you stay with us over Christmas."

"You know, I think I just might do that. I'll go home, get my overnight things and the presents for the family, and then I'll be right there."

"Good! I'm on my way to the bus depot to get Leigh, and then I'll be home."

My friend Leigh was coming from Vancouver to stay with us for the Christmas week. She was a good friend of ours, and she was looking forward to spending Christmas with the family. Leigh's bus arrived on schedule, and we arrived home just in time to meet Mom in the driveway.

తోఎ

I took Mom's suitcase to the spare bedroom and then made a pot of tea. We sat in the living room, talking and catching up on our day-to-day lives. Mom didn't look well. She had barely sipped her tea when she decided to go to her room to rest. She spent the remainder of the day in her room, which couldn't have been easy with the kids being so excited about Christmas.

Tess was ten and Nigel was seven years old. They were both thrilled at the thought of Santa coming the next morning.

We always spent Christmas Eve around the Christmas tree. It had been a long-standing tradition at our house to let the kids open one present that evening. The gift was the same item each year, and even though they knew what it was, they would still get excited.

They each opened their present to find a new pair of pajamas. After jumping up and down and giving lots of grateful hugs, they enthusiastically ran into their bedrooms to change. Mom really enjoyed this time with the kids. When they came back into the room dressed in their pajamas, she let them open a couple more presents from the many she brought every year.

So, with the kids happy, Mom said she was ready to go to bed. Her flu symptoms were not getting any better.

"I hope I feel better tomorrow for Christmas dinner and can eat something," she said. The doctor did say it's probably just the twenty-four hour flu. I sure hope he's right."

Mom went to bed and the kids were next. Finally, after much excitement and a fair bit of resistance, the kids went off to dreamland. Once they were fast asleep, I went down to the basement and retrieved our suitcases that were filled with wrapped presents. I was quite proud of myself for my ingenious hiding place. It had never entered the kids' minds to look inside the suitcases while they were secretly hunting for their Christmas gifts. It had worked for years.

My husband Corky and I finished the last-minute Christmas preparations and once the presents were under the tree, we too went to bed.

＆ペ

We were awakened before dawn by squeals of delight and scrambling footsteps tearing up the stairs.

"It's Christmas! Santa was here and he left tons of presents!" shrieked Nigel. "Quick, come downstairs!"

The morning went by quickly, with paper ripping and flying in the air. Once all the presents had been opened, Corky and the kids settled into the morning, reading instructions and assembling the many toys the kids had received.

Around noon, I began feeling a bit uneasy. Mom hadn't seemed to be any better from the day before. I knew she was putting up a good front for Christmas, but even so, shortly after opening the presents, she went to lie down in her room. That had been over three hours ago.

Mom and I had always made Christmas dinner together, since I was a child. She was the chief cook and I was her helper. However, it was becoming clear that this Christmas was going to be different. I was getting anxious because it looked like I might have to prepare the turkey and put it in the oven without her.

I felt a little foolish. Here I was, forty years old and nervous about cooking a turkey. Mom had always done it with such ease and confidence, and I hoped I could do the same. So I forged on. Leigh and I peeled the vegetables and prepared everything for the Christmas meal.

In the early afternoon, Mom finally came out of the bedroom. I could tell that she was really feeling under the weather.

I asked, "How are you, Mom? Can I get you anything— something to eat or drink?"

"No thanks," Mom answered. "I don't think I should put anything in my stomach right now. I'll just have to get through this, I guess. What a stupid time to get sick!"

"Come to think of it, you're hardly ever sick," I said. "I can't remember the last time you were like this."

"Yes, one thing I've always prided myself on is rarely being ill."

"Well, Mom, I guess a person has to be sick once in awhile. Don't worry about dinner. Leigh and I have it under control, but can you do me one favor? Can you check the turkey in the oven and make sure I've done everything right?"

To my relief, she said that it was coming along beautifully.

As dinner time was approaching, my father-in-law, Archie, arrived along with my brother-in-law Chris and his partner Eunice. Shortly after their arrival, we sat down to a perfect turkey dinner.

Archie and Mom sat beside each other at the dinner table. They had always enjoyed spending time together, and for years, I suspected that Archie secretly had a crush on Mom. They seemed to be having a good time except that Mom had hardly touched her food. I made a mental note to make a special meal for her when she was feeling better.

After dinner and the clean-up, we sat in the living room holding our stomachs and groaning that we ate too much. We were all tired from the long but exciting day, so the night came to an end and we all retired early to bed.

As I was tucking Tess in, she said, "That was the best Christmas I've ever had." She gave me a big hug and said good night. I walked into Nigel's room to find him barely awake. He mumbled a very sleepy good night. I knew he'd had a good time too.

I looked back on the day and thought about Mom. She must have been really sick to have gone to see the doctor. I knew that she was feeling a lot worse than she was letting on, yet she had hardly complained throughout the Christmas festivities. If only I had known then that there was so much more to her being ill. If only I had paid more attention to the signs, then maybe my life would be different today.

Chapter 2

I awoke early on Boxing Day morning. The first thought that came to mind was what a great day yesterday had been—it was one of the best Christmases ever, even with Mom feeling ill. It had been nice having her stay with us for the past two days, and I hoped she was feeling better today.

What made this Christmas different from the rest was that Mom now lived only a mile away. She had just recently retired at the age of sixty-nine from a managerial position at a bookstore in Kamloops and had finally moved back to Vernon after fifteen years of being away.

Even though Kamloops was only seventy miles away from Vernon, it wasn't always easy to visit her. To be able to see her now on a regular basis had to be the best Christmas present I had received this year. Mom was a big part of our family, and through the years we had tried to spend as much time together as we could.

I began craving a cup of coffee, so I jumped out of bed to go make it. But as I was walking by the downstairs bathroom to go to the kitchen, I stopped dead in my tracks, stunned. There were brown splash marks all over the toilet, the floor, and the bathroom door. I couldn't believe what I was seeing.

I walked around the house looking for some indication as to what had happened and found Mom lying on the living room couch. She was in intense pain, covered in sweat, and grimacing in agony. There was a distinct green color around her mouth, showing through ghostly white skin.

I hurried to her side. "Mom, what's wrong? What happened?"

She said, "I just threw up. Oh God, I'm in so much pain! It's my stomach!"

I yelled for Corky to come quickly. He raced out of the bedroom, took one look at Mom, and said, "Quick, we have to get Anne to the hospital!"

I grabbed Mom's clothes, helped her dress, and asked Leigh to stay with the kids while we were gone. We rushed Mom to the Emergency Unit at the hospital. She was in agony, moaning and breathing heavily. I begged the on-call physician to give her something for the pain. He came back with a syringe and gave Mom an injection of pain medication.

The doctor said gravely, "You have one very sick mother here. We're going to admit her to the hospital and run a battery of tests right away."

A while later, the doctor came into the room and said to Mom, "Anne, the x-rays show that you have a bowel blockage. We're going to try and drain your stomach to see if we can clear it."

৯৽৽৩

For the next two days, Mom was hooked up to tubes that went through her nostrils and into her stomach to try and drain the blockage. It was difficult to see her like this. She had just begun her new life in Vernon, renewing old friendships and enthusiastically decorating her newly-purchased home.

Mom had always been physically strong and was rarely ever sick. Through the years, we had been impressed by her stamina and would tease her that it was all that haggis she ate when she was young that kept her so healthy. But all kidding aside, we would often say it was her positive attitude toward life. For Mom, the glass was always half full. She didn't let things get her down.

৯৽৽৩

I spent the next few days keeping Mom company while she was in the hospital. We reminisced and talked a lot about her early years.

Mom was born and raised in Glasgow, Scotland. At the age of fifteen, she and her family moved to London where she finished high school at the age of seventeen and shortly thereafter began nursing training.

A few months after she started school, she met a handsome

twenty-year-old Canadian soldier named Leif Fagervik. He was a member of the Seaforth Highlanders of Canada and was stationed in Britain before his deployment to Italy in 1943.

Mom reminisced, "I remember the day I met my first husband, Leif. The minute I set eyes on him, I knew I was going to marry him. It was love at first sight, and we married just after my eighteenth birthday. We had been happily wed just seventeen months when he was killed in action near Salerno, Italy, on October 17, 1943. He was only twenty-one when he was buried at the Moro River Canadian War Cemetery, near where he was killed. I always wished that I could have visited his gravesite."

Mom continued, "I will never forget the day I received that terrible, impersonal telegram informing me of Leif's death. It is without a doubt one of the worst days of my life. I still have the telegram in a box in my closet, along with all his pictures."

I said, "I remember you showing me the telegram years ago. I think what touched me the most was seeing your tear drops that had permanently stained the paper. You were so young and so in love. It must have been devastating for you."

"Yes, I was devastated. I just couldn't believe that this had happened."

Mom sighed and said, "I'm not sure that I have ever stopped loving him."

"You know, I picked up on that when I was around twelve years old. I had always sensed that Leif had been the true love of your life and that you hadn't gotten over losing him."

Mom sheepishly said, "Oh dear, I didn't realize it was that obvious."

These talks reminded me of the many Sunday night dinners during my childhood spent listening to stories of London during World War II. I used to be amazed at how much danger Mom had faced and how brave she had been.

Mom went on, "Shortly after Leif's death, I decided that I wanted to make a contribution to the war effort, so I joined the Women's Army Corps as a nursing assistant. After the D-Day invasion, I found myself in a squad with the British Army as it pushed overland. We lived in tents for over eleven months. We followed behind the front lines, moving through Northern France into Belgium and finally into Northern Germany, where we ended up at the Bergen-Belsen concentration camp just as the war was ending."

Mom took a deep breath, "The worst thing that I have ever experienced in my life was witnessing the horror of that place. We discovered tens of thousands of prisoners inside who were very ill and starving. There were also thousands of unburied corpses lying around the camp. You could smell death from miles away. Honestly, Carole, just thinking about it makes me shudder. I will never understand how anyone can treat another human being like that."

"I can't imagine how shocking that must have been."

At that moment, the nurse walked over to Mom and checked her vital signs. It seemed to me that she left the room with a look of concern, and I wondered if I had read her reaction correctly. My thoughts were interrupted by Mom telling more stories of her adventures in the army.

"This one time, we set up our tents in a field in France," she continued. "On the evening of the fourth day, we had just finished dinner when I noticed that one of the flaps needed to be tightened on the tent. As I was standing on a hot wood stove fixing the flap, the air-raid sirens went off. I froze in fear and I found that I couldn't move. I thought, Oh my God, we are being air attacked! When I finally came out of my daze, I had burned the soles right off of my shoes!"

We laughed at this, and shaking her head, Mom went on. "Another time, we were being bombed by German planes in the early evening, near dusk, and I was ordered to use the anti-aircraft guns to shoot at the planes in the sky."

I stopped her in disbelief, saying, "But Mom, you are only five-foot-nothing. That must have been so hard to do!"

She said, "Well, you do what you are told when you are in the army, so I did it—with help, of course. You know, as awful as war is and as awful as it was trying to shoot down those planes, I remember

8

it was one of the most beautiful sights to see in the evening sky. The tracer bullets gave off a very intense white light that streaked across the sky as they flew through the air.

"Kind of like fireworks?" I asked.

"Yes, just like that. It was an exciting and amazing time in my life. Looking back, in a weird kind of way it was one of the best times in my life. There was real camaraderie. We all worked together for a common cause. We lived in the moment because, really, all we had was *that* moment. We would go to bed each night not knowing if we would wake up in the morning. We lived each day to its fullest. It's hard to believe I was only twenty-one years old!"

"Well, I now understand why I was raised so liberally," I mused. "I see why you never worried about me running all over the neighborhood way past dark. After all, you survived a war, so everything else must have seemed so safe!"

She laughed and said, "Yes, it was a very wild time back then. In May 1946, a year after the war ended, I had saved enough money to visit Leif's family in Canada for six weeks. It was an exciting adventure. I sailed on the Queen Mary, a most beautiful ship then and a very famous one now. What a wonderful journey that was. I still have the menus and napkins from the ship in my memento box."

She sighed happily, "I remember dancing the nights away in the ballroom night after night. I had so much fun, and even though I was by myself, everyone was so inclusive and friendly.

I finally arrived at my destination, the city of Halifax. From there, I took a train across Canada to Vernon. It was so wonderful meeting Leif's family but very sad also. His family was so warm and welcomed me with open arms. They were so happy to meet me and embraced me with so much love. I guess because I was Leif's wife, they felt close to him through me."

She paused and said, "Two weeks into my visit, as destiny would have it, the bank lost my money in transit for well over a month. I had very little cash left, so I had to find a job. During this time, I met your Dad, decided to stay in Vernon, and a year later married him and made my home in Canada."

I added, "And the rest is history."

Just at that moment, the spell was broken. The doctor came into the room to tell Mom that they would have to operate to find out why her bowel wouldn't release. He wanted to take her to the operating room immediately.

We were both surprised this was happening with so little notice. I looked at Mom and I could see that she was scared, but she didn't say anything. As I searched for the right words to console her, I reached for her hand and said, "Mom, you're going to be fine. They'll free the blockage and you'll be back to your old self again."

"I know. I'll be fine. I don't want you to worry about me."

At the time, we really did believe that she would be fine, that it really was only a blockage, and that it would just take this procedure to get everything in working order again.

I walked beside Mom's bed as they wheeled her to the door of the operating room. I gave her a hug, told her I loved her, and turned to wave good bye as I walked away.

The hospital staff told me that I might as well go home because they weren't sure how long the surgery would take. They would call me with the results. They said that once she was out of the operating room, she would be heavily sedated and would probably sleep through the night.

Driving home, I was a feeling a bit stunned at this new turn of events. Little did I know that this one event would change everything in my life and, for that matter, the lives of many people around me.

ৡৢ

Shortly after 8 p.m. that same evening, I received the expected call from Mom's surgeon. My intuition was telling me that this wasn't going to be good news.

He quietly began, "I'm sorry to have to tell you this Carole, but we found a large, cancerous tumor that was obstructing your Mother's bowel. Unfortunately, her intestine ruptured before the operation.

My mind went numb, was I hearing this correctly? There was a brief pause, and then he continued, "I have removed the tumor and I feel that all of the cancer is out of the bowel, but I'm afraid it has spread to her liver. And with liver cancer, there really isn't a lot of hope."

What! I couldn't believe what I was hearing. The doctor's telling me Mom has cancer and there is very little hope? That had never entered my mind.

I managed to ask, "How much time does she have left?"

"Well," the doctor paused, "I would say she has maybe a year at the very most."

A lump was forming in my throat, and I could not go on. I said, "I'm sorry, please give me a moment to collect myself. I will call you right back."

I was overwhelmed by this news. Not once had we ever thought Mom had cancer. That was such a nasty word, the "big C" word. I was completely stunned. As I hung up, my husband found me crying in the living room.

"What happened," he asked. "What did the doctor say?"

I could hardly answer. I whispered, "The surgeon has just told me Mom has terminal cancer. I didn't ask many questions. I just hung up. I need time to process this and collect myself. I'll phone him back in a minute and talk to him again."

I took a deep breath, pulled myself together and phoned the surgeon. I apologized, "I'm sorry I couldn't talk just now, but this is such shocking news. When can we see my mom? Should we come to the hospital now?"

"No, there is no point. She is heavily sedated and wouldn't know you were here anyway. Come in the morning when most of the anesthetic will have worn off. Just get a good night's sleep," he added.

I hung up, thinking, Get a good night's sleep? Is he serious?

I went to bed and quietly cried myself to sleep. I remember waking up a few times that night and finding that I had been crying in my sleep. I was surprised how hard it was for me to stop the tears. It was as if there were years of pent-up emotion flowing out of me.

The thought that Mom would not be with us for very much longer was unbearable.

¾S

At seven o'clock the next morning, I drove to the hospital. I was very concerned about whether or not Mom knew she had cancer. I was positive she would be devastated by this terrible news.

I rang the bell beside the door of the Intensive Care Unit. A minute went by, and then a tall, dark-haired nurse opened the door and let me in. Walking to Mom's room, I asked the nurse if the doctor had been in to see her yet and if so, had he told her that she had cancer? She said the doctor had just left, and yes, he had given her the bad news.

I paused, took a deep breath and went into Mom's room to see her. She looked so vulnerable.

I said as brightly as I could muster, "Hi, Mom. How are you feeling?"

She groggily said, "I am fine, much better now."

I sighed. As usual, my mother was always fine, no matter what happened. I sat down on the chair beside the bed and reached over to hold Mom's hand. I could not bring up the subject of cancer. I would remain quiet until she wanted to discuss it. I could see that Mom was far from being out of the woods. This operation had really taken a toll on her. She seemed to be having a hard time even staying conscious.

The nurse came in, and sensing my despair she put her hand on my shoulder and told me not to worry. She said that older people often have difficulty shaking the anesthetic. I felt a bit of relief from her kind words. Things had all happened so fast. It was such a shock. Everything all seemed so surreal.

I sat in Mom's room throughout that day and stayed on into the evening. She mostly slept and didn't talk much at all. Finally, around ten o'clock that evening, I went home very exhausted and feeling quite depressed. I gave my husband a quick hug and went right to bed.

I was in a very deep sleep when I awoke to the sound of the

telephone ringing early the next morning. It was the nurse in charge of Mom in the Intensive Care Unit. She told me that Mom was really disoriented and wouldn't let the nurses touch her or put the oxygen hose up to her nose because she thought they were trying to gas her.

"What!" I said, "That's not like Mom. Is she heavily medicated?"

"No, it's not the medication. As I mentioned to you yesterday, older people can react like this to anesthetics and to complicated surgeries like your mother has just had. It usually wears off in a day or so."

I woke my husband and said, "I have to go to the hospital right now because Mom's having trouble with the anesthetic. It's made her very disoriented and she is being cantankerous."

I arrived at the hospital within the hour. To my surprise, I found Mom sitting in a chair beside her bed.

I gave her a kiss on the cheek and asked, "What's the matter, Mom? Why are you arguing with the nurses?"

"They're trying to kill me. They're putting this air in my nose and it's a poisonous gas!" She had taken the hose out of her nose and was holding it tightly in her hand. She passed it over to me, saying, "Here, smell it. You will see I'm right!"

She was so mad. She was in a real fighting mood, and I wasn't sure how much help I was going to be in convincing her that the nurses were not going to kill her.

I smelled the oxygen hose and coaxingly said, "Mom, it's just oxygen, and the nurses say you need it. It will help you breathe more easily."

Mom sarcastically responded, "What do they know? I want to see the doctor. I want to get out of here, now!"

"Mom, look," I continued, "it's early. The doctor will be doing his rounds in an hour or so. You've just had major surgery, and you need to let the nurses take care of you. You can't leave here yet. You're still very sick."

Mom responded angrily, "So you're on their side! I asked the nurse to phone you because I thought you would help me, but you're no good to me. Why don't you go home? I'll keep them away myself," she said, with a very stubborn look on her face.

I tried to console her, but it wasn't much use. She wouldn't talk to me anymore. I was really shaken by this new behavior and really didn't know what to say or do at this point, so I just sat quietly beside her. A short time later, the nurse came into the room and asked me to help get Mom back into her bed. Once she was settled, she assured me again that this behavior would soon pass.

By early afternoon, Mom's health began declining rapidly. She had developed a high fever, and her chest made gurgling sounds with each breath she took.

At around 4 p.m., the doctor told me that they discovered she had peritonitis from the ruptured bowel. Peritonitis is an inflammation of the peritoneum, the tissue that lines the inner wall of the abdomen. On top of this, she had developed pneumonia, and her lungs were filling up with fluid. He wasn't sure she was going to make it with these additional health problems stacking up alongside the complicated surgery.

I was in shock. How could this be? Mom had had such a fighting spirit in the morning. How could things have changed so quickly? It was only a few days ago that we thought all she had was the flu! Was Christmas day just four days ago? It seemed so much longer than that now.

I phoned my brother Vern and his wife, Sandy, and told them to come as quickly as they could to see Mom. They arrived the next day to find her in a very poor state. We spent the next two days in Mom's room, taking turns staying with her day and night and hoping that she would get through this crisis.

My brother Vern is four years older than me, and because of our age difference, we hadn't spent a lot of time together when we were growing up. He joined the Navy and left home when I was thirteen years old, and we didn't see much of each other after that. Spending these many hours together at the hospital gave us the opportunity to get to know one another. We reminisced about the crazy things we used to do when we were children and what an easy-going and fun Mom we had while we were growing up.

The next two days went by in a blur. Mom was declining. The doctors could not find the right antibiotic for her stomach infection, and the pneumonia was getting worse. Her lungs were filling up with fluid at a rapid rate. The doctor said that we would have to put her on life support to keep her alive and that we, as a family, had to make some important decisions about whether we wanted to let her go or try to save her.

The doctor advised us that efforts shouldn't be made to keep her alive because she had liver cancer, and in the future, she would only have to suffer more.

We are not a religious family, but we went into a private waiting room and prayed to do the right thing for Mom. We came to the conclusion that we would let Mother Nature make that choice.

It was a very hard decision, but in the end, we told the doctors that we would like to keep Mom off any life-support equipment. The doctor said that they would drain her lungs periodically to keep her comfortable but that was all they would do. So with everything in place, we braced ourselves for the inevitable.

Early the next morning, my brother and I arrived at the hospital to find the doctor in the room with Mom. He informed us that she had taken a turn for the worse and that she had no more than two or three hours to live. My brother looked at me with deep pain and sadness in his eyes and suddenly broke down. With his face in his hands, crying, he stumbled over to me and hugged me. I held him and whispered, "I know it's not much of a consolation right now, but we will have each other, Vern."

I felt numb at the thought that Mom would soon be gone. It was all happening too quickly. She was not ready to die and I was not ready to lose her. She had so much to live for: following through on her long-awaited retirement plans for travelling, being with the family (especially her grand-children), golfing, and just all round enjoying life. It was so unfair.

I walked over to Mom's bedside and held her hand.

She softly whispered, "I have to go now. I'm leaving."

I quietly said, "I love you, Mom. Please don't go, please try and live. We can't lose you now."

Mom kept her eyes closed, smiled a beautiful smile, and again said, "I'm leaving. The golden light around me is so beautiful, and I want to go home."

Perplexed, I asked, "Go home?" What do you mean?"

She happily replied, "Leif is here and he has come to take me home."

Up to a few days ago, Mom hadn't mentioned Leif's name in over twenty-five years, and now she was talking about him again. I knew that she had really loved Leif; as she had said, he was the love of her life.

I didn't know what to say to her at this moment. I had heard about people who've had a near-death experience, and I wondered if this was happening to Mom now.

Reluctantly I whispered, "It's all right Mom, you go."

She said, "I love you and I will see you again. Where I am going is so wonderful. I'm going with Leif. He has been waiting for me for fifty years. He loves me very much, and he's come to take me home. I'm sorry. I won't be able to talk to you anymore."

I said, "That's okay, Mom. I love you. You go to Leif."

She had a beautiful smile on her face and glowed with happiness. She whispered, "I love you. Goodbye."

I too was smiling but crying at the same time. It was strange, but I felt very happy for Mom. I was glad she was not alone in her dying and that she would be reunited with Leif. It seemed that her death was not as ominous as I thought. She was so willing to go.

I walked out of Mom's room and spoke with the nurse about what I had just experienced.

She said, "It is quite common for Intensive Care Unit patients to have loved ones from the other side come to them while they are in the process of dying. Some have a near-death experience and survive to tell their story."

She went on, "There are many accounts of patients leaving their bodies and upon resuscitation, talking about the procedures being done to save their lives. Many patients over the years have told me they left their bodies and watched from above while the medical staff hovered around them."

I thanked the nurse for her reassuring words and then went back into Mom's room and sat in the chair beside her bed. Her breathing was shallow and slow. Reaching out for her hand, I wondered if she was really with Leif. As I pondered this thought, the nurse came into the room and called Mom by her name. To my surprise, she opened her eyes. I was confused; did she decide not to leave? Was it just a flight of the imagination on Mom's part? This was puzzling, but at the same time, I was very relieved that she was still with us for the moment.

Chapter 3

It was New Year's Eve. We'd had a tradition where we went to dinner with three families at the local ski hill and then brought in the New Year by playing Charades at a friend's cabin, but unfortunately that wasn't going to happen this year. I knew the kids would be disappointed, but we needed to be close to the hospital; so instead, we all went for a quick dinner at a restaurant in town. I would have missed dinner altogether, but I didn't want to let the kids down on New Year's.

Immediately after finishing our meal, Corky took the kids home, and Vern, Sandy and I went back to the hospital to be with Mom.

She was really struggling to stay alive. With her eyes still closed, she whispered, "I want to stay, but I'm in a dark hole. I can't get out of it. I don't know what to do, I'm stuck."

I wanted desperately to help her. I wanted to give her something to hold on to, and all I could think to say was, "Ask for help, Mom."

Mom wasn't alert for long. She went back into a coma-like state and didn't answer when we tried to converse with her.

Not knowing what else to do, Vern, Sandy and I put our hands on Mom and prayed to help her get through this crisis and give her more time to enjoy her life. We sat around her, quietly talking for the next few hours. It was nearing midnight when Vern and Sandy told me to go home and get some sleep.

Vern said, "Sandy and I are going to sleep here tonight, so don't worry. You need a break, and I promise we'll phone you if anything happens."

Mom had been in the Intensive Care Unit for a week. I had spent more time at the hospital than at home. Corky and the kids had barely seen me and I felt a bit guilty. I couldn't remember having a full night's sleep in a long while. This offer was something I wasn't going to refuse, so I made them promise that they would call me at the slightest change in Mom.

I drove home craving my bed and fell asleep before my head hit my pillow.

☙◦❧

I awoke early the next morning. I hadn't heard from Vern, which was a big relief. I jumped out of bed, got ready as quickly as I could, and decided to pick up a coffee on the way to the hospital in order to save time. When I got to Mom's room, I found a very exhausted brother and sister-in-law. It was my turn to tell them to go home and get some sleep.

I was surprised to find that Mom had rallied somewhat and seemed a little better. She was far from being out of the danger zone, but her eyes were open and she was a bit more talkative and seemed less confused.

I asked, "Mom, do you remember you said you were leaving with Leif, and you said goodbye to us? Why didn't you leave with him?"

She was silent for a long time and then said, "I could have left if I had wanted, but Leif said that there was still more things that I could experience before I went over to the other side. I did have a choice. I could have gone home, but I decided to stay because there is still more for me to do here. Leif told me that he would be waiting for me and would come and get me when my time to die came around again."

I held her hand and said, "I'm so glad that you didn't leave. I know you can beat this, Mom. You just have to keep fighting."

Mom seemed so much better, but the doctor's prognosis still wasn't that good. He was uncertain whether she would get over this rough patch and felt that she could go either way. My intuition, however, was telling me that Mom would make it: she had made a conscious decision to live.

As the days went by, she slowly appeared to be on the road to recovery and was definitely feeling better. I spent every moment I could by her bedside, talking when she felt up to it and reading when she slept.

Gradually, she began to eat foods like Jell-O and then slowly progressed to more solid food, which consisted of cream soups and puddings.

The one thing that continued to be disturbing was that she would vomit shortly after eating. The doctor said that it was caused either by the anesthetic, the operation itself, or the aftermath of the stomach infection. They decided to administer anti-nausea medication before every meal but that didn't seem to work very well. It just slowed down the time before Mom got sick, but inevitably she would still vomit.

By this time, Mom had spent two weeks in the Intensive Care Unit. At the beginning of the third week, the doctor transferred her to the regular ward as she had stabilized and was doing fairly well.

Vern and Sandy had to get back to work. The doctor assured them that Mom was improving daily and that the worst was behind her. With the doctor's prognosis, they felt confident that she was in good hands, so they made the decision to drive back to Victoria the next day.

෨ෛ

Mom hit the one-month mark of her illness and was still in the hospital recuperating. This was the longest month that both she and I had ever spent.

On one of those long days, I finally found the courage to ask Mom if she had known that she was sick with something much worse than the flu but hadn't wanted to admit it.

She looked upset and said, "I was so foolish, Carole. Yes, I knew something was wrong back in November, but I was afraid to go to the doctor. I guess I knew deep inside that I was in trouble but I ignored the symptoms, hoping they would go away."

She continued, "A few days before Christmas, I finally broke down and went to the doctor about the bloating in my stomach and told him that I didn't feel well. He told me I had the same flu that everyone in town was coming down with and that I should go home and rest. I liked his explanation. I felt relieved and I wanted to believe his diagnosis."

As I listened to what Mom was saying, I was surprised at my reaction. I began to seethe inside. I was mad at the doctor and I was mad at Mom. I could feel my frustration rise.

I questioned Mom, "Why did you listen to the doctor and that diagnosis? You said you knew something was wrong. You should have asked him to do some tests because if you had, you wouldn't be in this predicament today. At least your bowel wouldn't have ruptured."

I paused, took a breath and went on, "They probably would have found the tumor by giving you an ultra-sound or an x-ray, and you wouldn't have had all these complications to deal with."

Mom's eyes flashed in anger. "I know I should have done something a long time ago. It's too late. There is nothing I can do about it now."

I couldn't help myself. I was so frustrated. I continued, "You know, Mom, you should have been having bowel check-ups every five years. You know very well there's a family history of bowel cancer. Both your dad and brother died from it, and it's just lucky for your sister that she beat it."

She said, "I know. I know I was stupid. I was worried that once the doctors got hold of me, they'd just keep cutting."

I wanted to shout, "Well, what do you think just happened, Mom?" but I bit my tongue and didn't say anything.

We both sat in silence, mad at each other. I could not help myself, but for my part, I wanted to yell, "How could you be so stupid? How could you do this to us?" I took some deep breaths, calmed myself down, got up out of my chair, and gave Mom a hug. I did not want to hurt her any more than she had already been hurt.

After this disagreement, I knew that Mom was already mad enough at herself without my criticizing her any further. I wouldn't bring it up again. With a soft voice, I said, "You're right, Mom. There is no point in crying over spilt milk. Let's just focus on getting you better now; that's what counts. You've made some really big steps toward getting well again, especially making the decision to quit smoking since your operation."

Mom answered, "Well, it's been tough, I really miss it, but I've made a promise to myself that I'll never smoke again. I wouldn't doubt that cigarette smoking is one of the reasons I got cancer."

Day after day, I sat with Mom in the hospital. She wanted to go home, but it wasn't possible because she still had a lingering infection in her abdomen. The incision had split open in two places and was draining out brown and green pus. The dressings had to be changed three to four times a day.

One of the most difficult parts of this entire illness was the temporary colostomy bag that had been placed in Mom's abdomen. Because the bowel had ruptured, the surgeon had to let it rest, but he hoped that he could reconstruct it in three months' time and reverse the colostomy.

The nurse had taught Mom how to change the bag, but she still found it very difficult to master. The nurse assured Mom that she wasn't alone; that many patients had a hard time with the technique, but she was certain that Mom would get the hang of it soon enough. One of the worst complications of having the bag was that it frequently leaked. This was extremely humiliating, and she couldn't wait until it was reversed. She was putting a lot of effort into gaining the extra twenty pounds that she needed before they would operate on her again.

ॐॐ

The days began to flow one into the next. I could see that it was really getting to Mom having to sit in her bed day after day, with no definite answers as to when she could leave the hospital. The frustration was there, but she still didn't complain or get angry. I would often wonder how she kept up such a good attitude with all that she had endured. I knew that if it were me, I wouldn't have been able to tolerate the many hardships that she had gone through in the past six weeks without complaining an awful lot.

Finally, on day fifty-one, the dam burst. Mom couldn't take it anymore and she broke down. She began to sob and with enormous frustration, she vented, "I have to get out of here! I lie here day in and day out with nothing to do. My God, how much more can I take?"

I went over and hugged her as her frail body shook from sobbing. "I wish you could get out of here too, Mom."

Just as I was handing Mom a tissue, the nurse came into the room and said, "I couldn't help hearing what you just said, Anne. I don't see any reason why you can't go home. The home care nurses can take care of your incision now and can do the same thing we're doing. I'll phone the doctor and try to get you released from here as soon as possible."

Mom blew her nose and wiped her tears.

I said, "I agree, the nurse is right. It's time to get out of here."

Finally, on February 16, the doctor told Mom she could go home, but she was not allowed to be alone. She was still too weak to get around by herself and needed someone to care for her.

I told Mom that she could stay with us, that we would love to have her. She had a really difficult time agreeing to this, but she desperately wanted her freedom back. Our house looked a lot better than the hospital, so she conceded to the fact that she had to be with us for a while.

ھ‑ଙ

Having Mom stay at our house only lasted five days. She was determined to go to her own home and get on with her life, but there were many things that needed to be organized before she could be on her own.

I contacted home care services, and after a lot of planning, it was arranged that a home care nurse would come to Mom's house twice daily to take care of her incision. Homemakers would also come to Mom's house twice weekly. They would buy groceries and cook meals that would last throughout the week. As I organized these services, I was reminded of the article I had read in the paper about the study done on the cost of hospital care versus home care. The study proved that subsidized home care was more economical than keeping patients in the hospital. At that moment, I was very thankful that they had done that study.

With all the services in place, we took Mom home to her place. She was so happy to be back in her own house. I, on the other hand, was apprehensive about Mom being alone. I had become very protective of her.

Mom sat down on her living room couch and asked me to sit down beside her.

She said, "Carole, I don't want you to think that I don't appreciate everything you've done, but I want to get on with my life. I don't want you to worry. The doctor said that he removed all the cancer and I feel that he did, and now I'm going to work at getting well again."

"I'm just glad you are on the mend and that you are happy being back home," I replied. "I do think you are going to get well again. It's just going to take some time, and I will be here for you whenever you need anything. I'm just a phone call away."

I really didn't want to believe that Mom had any cancer left either, and to tell the truth, I had really convinced myself at this time that she was cancer free. So there we were, both in denial and both really believing that everything would be just fine again. Little did we know how wrong we were.

Chapter 4

By the end of April, Mom's health had improved significantly. She'd kept the promise to never smoke again and was winning the battle after fifty-three years. She readily admitted that she regretted smoking and wished she had quit years ago. We were impressed by her determination to stay away from cigarettes as it couldn't have been easy.

Gaining weight for Mom was still a challenge. Along with her meals, she added high-calorie fruit smoothies that were specifically made for gaining weight. The drinks were tasty, and Mom was slowly putting weight on again. She still had times when she couldn't keep food down, but this was happening less often so we didn't give it too much thought.

Now that she had fully recovered from her surgery and her strength had returned, she began driving her car again. Mom was over the moon about her new found freedom as it gave back that much wanted—and needed—independence that had been so desperately missed during her illness.

I felt very positive about Mom at this time. My life was slowly resuming its normal pace, and my family was happy to have me back. I frequently received calls from Mom telling me her eventful schedule; she was going to lunch, to the mall shopping, or out for dinner with friends. She was keeping very busy.

On a number of occasions, she would mention that she was sure that she didn't have any cancer left; that the doctor really didn't know for sure there was cancer in her liver, and that she, herself, was pretty sure he was wrong. Actually, she was completely convinced he was wrong. I often felt little twinges of anxiety when she talked like this. I wondered if I should remind her that the doctor had told her he was quite certain that her liver had been affected by cancer. I knew that she was in denial. She was refusing to accept it, and, quite honestly, I didn't want to accept it either. I wanted to believe that she would be just fine; that after she got her colostomy reversed she would have won the uphill battle.

It seems bizarre to me now, looking back, how easy it was to pretend that this terrible ordeal with cancer was in the past; that the worst was over, and life would soon return to normal.

☙ ❧

It was the beginning of May. Mom had an appointment with the surgeon to get the prognosis on reversing her colostomy. Over four months had passed since the operation at Christmas. Mom was on tenterhooks as she sat in the office, hoping she was a candidate for this procedure. She was thrilled when the surgeon gave her the good news that she had gained enough weight to be able to have another surgery. This required Mom to go through the same procedure that she had undergone in December. The operation was booked for May 14.

As I was driving Mom home from the doctor's visit, she said, "You know, I'm not that nervous about the operation. I'm just relieved that I won't have to deal with these horrible bags any more. They have come apart and leaked so many times in public." She went on, "Remember when we were standing in line at the bank and the bag partially came off and began to leak?"

She shook her head as she said, "I think one of the worst times this happened was when I was having lunch with Cathy in my white slacks, and before I could do anything, there were brown stains all down the front of me." She took a deep breath and said, "I am just so damn tired of the constant worry and embarrassment. I'm at the point where I don't want to go out in public or even socialize at all anymore."

"Well Mom, thank heavens you won't have to worry about that much longer; the operation is less than a week away and that annoying bag will be gone."

"Yes, we should have a big party after!" Mom said jokingly.

"Speaking of parties," I said, "we want to take you out to dinner tomorrow evening for Mother's Day. The restaurant is really lovely and the food is excellent. Can we pick you up around five o'clock?"

"Oh, that sounds great! I look forward to that. Any time is fine with me."

∾∾

The next evening we arrived at the restaurant for Mother's Day. We ordered a glass of wine and had a toast to the upcoming reversal of her colostomy and to a new and healthy life.

Encouragingly I said, "Mom, don't fret about the operation. It won't be as bad as what you went through before; your bowel won't rupture this time, so you won't get peritonitis or pneumonia. The only thing you'll have to recuperate from is the actual operation and maybe the anesthetic."

"Well, I hope you're right. I realize that I am so fortunate that I can get this colostomy reversed. Since I've had this bag, I've talked to a few people who've had similar health problems to me, but, unfortunately, they have to wear a bag for the rest of their lives. I had no idea what a person goes through with a colostomy until now. It's been quite an eye opener."

Corky said, "We had no idea either, I guess we've all learned a lot."

We changed the subject. Mom began sharing her plans for the future about all the things she was going to do once she was completely well again. Mom was her bubbly self. There was hope and enthusiasm in her words, and her eyes were sparkling with excitement. Life would soon be back to normal: her illness would be behind her and soon it would be a distant memory.

After a delicious dinner and a very enjoyable time, we drove Mom to her house. We made sure she was comfortable and then left for home.

On the way to our house, Corky and I talked about the up-coming operation. He was apprehensive and worried that it wasn't going to turn out as well as Mom and I were expecting. He didn't want to be negative, but he wanted me to be prepared for the possibility of bad news. We both hoped that she would make it through the operation better than she did the last time.

❧ ❧

May 14 arrived. It was the big day for the operation that would reverse Mom's colostomy. Walking into the hospital that early morning with Mom reminded me of how much I disliked being there. The place was way too familiar, and the smell was nauseatingly the same as it was before.

Mom's nerves were showing. Even though she was anxious and scared, she was determined to go through with the operation and get rid of the colostomy bag.

We walked into Mom's hospital room on the surgical floor. There were four beds, in all, and Mom's was by the window. Mom changed into a green hospital gown and then sat on the bed. I could see the anxiety and fear on her face.

I tried to be encouraging, "Mom, you're going to be fine. Just keep remembering that you won't be as sick as you were before."

She hesitantly answered, "I hope not. I don't think I would make it this time if I were. I just want all of this to be over, and the sooner the better."

The nurse came into the room and gave Mom two pills: one for nausea and the other a sedative. Mom swallowed them both.

A few minutes later, the nurse came back with a wheelchair and said, "Anne, it's time for you to go to the operating room. Would you like your daughter to wheel you down?"

"Yes, I would like that," she said.

I wheeled Mom to the door of the operating room. I could see that she was really getting anxious. She took a deep breath, looked at me with big brown eyes, and said, "Well, this is it. I hope I make it."

I gave her a kiss, and giving her lots of encouragement I said, "You're going to make it just fine; you wait and see. You will be awake before you know it."

She smiled weakly, looked down at her lap, and quietly said, "I sure hope so."

It was just before noon when the anesthetist walked over to us. He smiled at Mom and softly said that it was time to go. I gave Mom a hug and wished her good luck.

As I was driving home to have a quick lunch before going back to the hospital, I had concerns about the operation. I had a sense that something was not right. But I wanted to be positive, so I tried to shake the negative thoughts from my mind.

I arrived home and made myself a sandwich. Just as I was sitting down to eat, the phone rang. The ringing sounded more shrill than usual, and somehow I just knew there was bad news on the other end of the line. I was not sure I wanted to answer, yet I knew I had no choice.

It was only twelve thirty, so I optimistically thought that it couldn't possibly be the doctor. He had told me the operation would last at least two hours. I answered the phone, and unfortunately it was the surgeon.

He began, "Hi Carole." He paused and then said, "I am truly sorry to tell you this, but when I went in to reverse the colostomy, I found that the cancer has spread throughout your mom's abdomen and into her liver. I am sorry to say there isn't a lot of time left for your mom: maybe three to six months at the most."

I was numb, yet I was not surprised.

I said, "I hope you were you able to reverse the colostomy."

He said, "I am so sorry, but it was impossible because there is a tumor on top of her intestine, and I would have had to cut it out to proceed with the operation. Unfortunately that would have caused massive bleeding, and there was a good chance she would have died on the operating table."

"Oh no," I said, "She's going to be so upset. When can I come and see her?"

He said, "She should be coming out of the anesthetic soon. She was only under for a short time, so it won't take her long to come around. I am sure she'll be awake within the hour."

In a daze, I thanked the doctor and hung up the phone.

I don't know why, but at that moment, I felt more sorrow at the fact that Mom still had her colostomy than about finding out the cancer had spread throughout her abdomen. I guess I had suspected it all along, but didn't want to admit it. How was she going to take this? The thought that she had all those stitches again for nothing, and then to be told that she had six months to live at the most would be overwhelming for her. I felt hopelessly inadequate. This was so unfair. Why would this happen to someone like her?

Corky arrived home to have lunch minutes after I hung up from talking with the doctor. He took one look at my tear-stained face and said, "Oh boy, not good eh?"

With a lump in my throat I answered, "Nope, Mom's abdomen is full of cancer, and she has very little time left to live. I had better get to the hospital right away. She doesn't know any of this yet, and when she finds out, she's going to be devastated. Can you phone Vern and tell him he had better get here as soon as possible? I have to go and see Mom right away."

૎્

I arrived at the hospital and found Mom a little groggy from the anesthetic but surprisingly alert. I sat in the chair beside her, reached for her hand, and asked if the doctor had spoken to her about the results of the operation.

She answered, "No, he'll be in to see me in the morning."

I wondered why the doctor had not told her. Now I was going to have to be the one to give her the bad news.

Mom asked, "Is the colostomy reversed?"

I felt as though a rock had hit me in the stomach; I felt sick. How was I going to tell her this terrible news? I took a deep breath and said, "No Mom, they couldn't reverse the colostomy."

She lay quietly for a moment, clicked her tongue and then asked, "Why not?"

Oh God, how was I going to tell her all of this? I felt incapable and at a loss for the right words. Were there any right words for what I was going to have to say to her? This was the hardest thing that I had ever had to do: to give a virtual death sentence to my mother and best friend.

I swallowed hard. "Mom," I began, "the doctor said that when they opened you up, the cancer had spread throughout your abdomen. Metastasis, I think, is what he called it."

She clicked her tongue again. She was silent and then after a moment said, "What are we going to do now?"

I softly answered, "I don't know Mom. I'm so sorry this has happened to you."

She said, "Well I'm going to beat this thing. There has to be a way. What about chemotherapy?"

"The doctor told me that you can have chemotherapy, but he felt that you would only suffer more and probably get very sick. He said that because the cancer has gone to your liver, there was nothing more he could do. It was incurable. He thinks you should enjoy the time you have left and live as normal a life as you can under the circumstances."

I paused, "But, if you want chemotherapy, then you should have it."

Mom said, "I don't know what to do. I've seen people so sick having chemotherapy, and if I only have six months left, I don't want to spend all my time feeling ill."

"There are other possibilities, Mom. A friend of mine gave me a pamphlet the other day about a clinic in Mexico that's been working with cancer patients for fifty-five years. Supposedly, they have a fairly high success rate with treating cancer. I know it's a long shot, but it might be something to try."

I was surprised at Mom's quick decision. There was no hesitation whatsoever.

She said, "Okay. Can you come with me?"

I tentatively said, "Maybe you should check this clinic out a bit more before you make any kind of decisions, but saying that, of course I will come."

Mom said, "I've talked to a few people who have gone to Mexico and are doing quite well with alternative treatments. Find out as much as you can about the clinic and what we have to do to get there, then book our flights as soon as you can."

"Mom, hold on, not so fast! You're going to have to recuperate from this operation first."

"Don't worry. I'll be fine, but we have to get there as soon as possible. I don't have any time to play with anymore. I have to get on this."

I phoned my brother that evening to tell him that Mom was doing fairly well under the circumstances. She had not been under the anesthetic long enough for it to have affected her adversely.

I said, "Vern there is something that Mom wants to do. You're going to flip out, so you need to sit down. I took a deep breath and said, "You're not going to believe this, but Mom wants to go to a cancer clinic in Tijuana."

There was silence and then he said, "That's rather rash, don't you think? I mean, do you know anything about this clinic? How did she find out about this place?"

"Well, she found out from me, and I found out from a doctor here in Vernon. I've already phoned the clinic in Mexico, and they have explained what the protocol is.

"This is kind of crazy, don't you think?"

"I would say more desperate, if anything." I went on, "So what I know so far is that the clinic is in Tijuana, on the Mexican border, about twenty-five minutes from San Diego. I was told that because people come to the clinic from so many different parts the world, the clinic can only operate on a first come, first serve basis and cannot make pre-booked appointments. The patient has to be at the clinic before nine o'clock in the morning.

"Do people stay in Tijuana?"

"No, they provide a shuttle service from your hotel in San Diego to the clinic. Patients go for one day only and are then shuttled back at the end of the day."

"So Mom would only have to be in Mexico for one day."

"Yes, and then she can go back home the next day if she wants to. But I was thinking that if Mom's feeling okay, we can stay a few days longer and spend some quality time with her."

"I don't know. This is all so sudden. Look, I'll be at the hospital tomorrow around 5:00 p.m. We can talk about this proposed trip to Mexico then."

༓ ༓

Vern arrived at the hospital the following afternoon. He had barely walked into Mom's room before she brought up the subject of the Mexican clinic. She handed him the pamphlet and asked that he read it right away. He sat down beside her bed and read the information carefully.

He said, "Well, looking at this brochure, I think going to Mexico is worth a try."

I asked, "Could you come with us? I don't think we can do this without you."

He hesitated, "I'm not sure I can find the time. As you know, I've just started with a new real estate office and it's difficult for me to take time off."

We stared intensely at him not giving him an inch. Looking back at both of our pleading faces, he realized that he really had no choice but to come with us.

He sighed and said, "All right, you got me."

I jumped up, hugged him, and said, "This is great. I am so happy we will be doing this together."

Mom looked pleased and said, "Now, I just have to get out of here."

I knew this was a difficult decision for Vern. He had been a marine engineer in the navy for twenty years, and this change to working as a real estate broker was very different for him. But I was glad he was willing to take the time to go to Mexico.

The next day we went to the travel agent, bought the tickets to San Diego, and made reservations at a hotel on the waterfront. I was very anxious about being in the United States with no insurance for Mom. The insurance company would not insure her for any health problems related to cancer or her surgery. I worried that the incision might open and she could end up in an American hospital with an enormous medical bill.

In hindsight, we were bordering on madness and were completely irresponsible about the risk we were taking, but we were willing to do anything to try and find help for Mom.

Chapter 5

On May 29, two weeks after Mom's operation, we boarded the plane to San Diego. Surprisingly, Mom felt fairly well physically and her spirits were high. We had great expectations about this Mexican clinic, especially since this really was the only option we had.

The trip was long and tiring. We had to change planes twice: once in Vancouver and once in Portland. Finally, after seven hours of travel, we arrived at our hotel in San Diego in time for dinner. The hotel was beautiful, and our room was spacious with a gorgeous view of the harbor.

As soon as we had settled in our room, I phoned the lady in charge of transportation to the Mexican Clinic. She said that she would be outside the hotel the next morning, at eight o'clock sharp, to drive us to the clinic.

Just as I hung up the phone, Mom came out of the bathroom in her pajamas. She was exhausted. She told us that she wasn't hungry and insisted that Vern and I go for dinner without her. We were hungry, so we went to the rooftop lounge and chose seats next to the window. The view of the ocean was stunning. There were several navy ships in the harbor, and the sun was just beginning to set, giving the sky an exotic, tropical pink hue.

Vern said, "Man, what a day! I can't believe we're really here."

"I know. I can't either. Can you believe Mom's determination? My God, she just had a major operation two weeks ago and is doing so well. There's no comparison to the last time she had surgery. She's recuperated much faster than I would have imagined."

"Yes, she's really incredible. I hope this clinic is on the up-and-up and isn't out to scam us."

I said, "Your comment just reminded me that there's something I've been meaning to tell you. The day before we left, I spoke with a doctor who had been to the clinic a few years ago. He told me that the medical doctors at the clinic were very well trained. Some of the doctors were from the United States and some were from Mexico. He said that he had checked out five of the existing cancer clinics in Mexico, and this clinic was the best by far. He was impressed by the amount of success they were having with terminal cancer patients."

Vern said, "Well, I guess we'll see for ourselves tomorrow."

We sat quietly for a while. We both had the same feelings of skepticism mixed with hope. We trusted the doctor I spoke with was right.

လ•၆

Mom was the first to get out of bed the next morning. She had no intention of missing that ride to the clinic for any reason. We finished breakfast and walked outside the hotel at eight o'clock to find our driver, Mrs. Rodden, waiting to take us to the clinic. She was an American citizen who lived in San Diego and had worked for the clinic for several years.

We got into the van. It was obvious that we were very tense, and as we drove out of the parking lot of the hotel I began wondering if we were going on a wild goose chase. I remembered back to a few days earlier when a couple of friends of mine expressed that we were crazy to be going to Mexico to find a cure for cancer. They said that desperation leads a person to believe just about anything.

I had to admit, at that moment it did seem bizarre to be going to a "third-world" country looking for a cure for a disease. I really questioned at that time whether we had seriously lost our minds.

We soon arrived in Tijuana; a town I had never been to before. There were many shanties along the way, and the roads were full of pot-holes. Many of the buildings were run-down, but it didn't seem to be quite as bad as what I had heard about Tijuana.

We arrived at the clinic at twenty minutes before nine. We were in luck; they would take Mom as a patient that day. This was quite a relief as we didn't think we would be able to summon up the courage to ever come back again.

The clinic was in a large, white stucco house with tile floors. Looking around, I could see that it was completely different from what we were used to in Canada. Many patients were sitting in the waiting room in their hospital gowns, casually chatting to one another. In Canada, once a patient has changed out of their personal clothing, they sit in a private cubicle or room while waiting for the doctor. This was surprisingly informal.

Mom changed into her gown and laughingly said, "Well, there is no point in being shy. I guess I'll hang around in my gown too."

We had just sat down when a nurse asked Mom to come with her to another part of the clinic for blood tests, urine samples, and x-rays. Mom returned an hour later.

I asked, "So how was it, Mom?"

"Well it really wasn't that much different than hospitals in Canada. Everything looked sterile to me, and everyone seemed very professional."

"Oh, that's a relief. Let's hope we feel the same way about the doctors," I said.

By this time, we had been at the clinic for more than two hours. I was getting impatient, so I walked up to the receptionist and asked when Mom would be seeing the doctor. She told me that it was one of the busiest days that they had ever had; there were over twenty-five patients. She was sorry for the wait, but as soon as a doctor was free, Mom would be called.

Oh great, I thought, trust us to pick the busiest day ever!

I went back and told Mom what the receptionist had said.

Mom was a bit nervous and said, "I don't know about this place. Do you think it's reliable?"

"I don't know Mom, but don't worry. Let's just see what happens. We don't have to take any of their advice if we don't want to. Let's just try and keep an open mind."

A short time later, Mom's name was finally called to see the doctor. The clinic had requested that Mom bring all her medical records from Canada. So with all her information in hand, she disappeared down the hall and went into the doctor's office.

Close to an hour later, Mom finally returned. She said that she was really impressed by the physical exam that had been done;

she couldn't remember the last time she had been checked over so thoroughly. Mom sat down, saying that she had to stay at the clinic until the end of the day. The doctor wanted to see her one more time before she left.

It was going to be a long day, so while I was waiting, I thought I would talk with some of the patients and ask questions about the clinic. I was told that the doctors were from excellent medical schools; they were dedicated, well-trained doctors committed to curing cancer. Many of the patients were enthusiastic about the clinic and wanted to share what they had been through since they became ill.

The first lady I spoke with had come to the clinic from New York City. She had been given a grim sentence some eleven years earlier. Tumors had been found in both lungs, in her stomach, and under her collar bone. She was given two months, at the most, to live. In desperation, she had come to this clinic ten years before, and because of the treatment she'd received, she was completely clear of cancer. The reason she was at the clinic this time was that her daughter had now been diagnosed with cancer.

An eighty-six-year-old man from Florida spoke up at this time. He said that nine years earlier he had been diagnosed with stomach cancer and told that there was no hope. He had heard positive reviews about this clinic, so he came to get help. He had followed the clinic's treatment, and was also free of cancer. He was back for his yearly checkup. He trusted the doctors at this clinic more than the regular medical system back home.

Another lady from Los Angeles shared her experience with me. Two years earlier, she had been diagnosed with a tumor the size of a grapefruit in one of her breasts. Her doctor wanted to remove her breast, but she refused. The day after this diagnosis, she drove to the clinic. She was now completely clear of cancer and still had her breast. She, too, respected the doctors at the clinic and came to the clinic for checkups on a regular basis.

I talked with two men who had been diagnosed with skin cancer. One of the men, a number of years before, had had cancer on his forehead, just above his eyebrow. The doctor back home had wanted to operate, with a possibility that he would have to take the eye, along with the cancer. The other man had had skin cancer on his lower back. The doctor had also wanted to operate. Rather than have surgery, both men had come to the clinic to try alternative treatments. They had been in remission for over six years. They, too, were just down for check-ups.

At one point as I was listening to these stories, I wondered if these people had been hired by the clinic as actors. I know that was a crazy thought, but I had always believed that there were very few cures for cancer and many of these people had been diagnosed as being terminally ill. They were telling me that because of this clinic and its treatments, they were in remission—some for well over nine years. I found it very hard to believe.

Vern had been harboring fears, as well, about the clinic's credibility. When we first arrived, he voiced his concerns; but as the day progressed, he grew to see that the staff was well-trained and very sincere. Patients were clear of cancer. There really was something to this place, and if it could happen for them, why not for Mom?

Many patients that day told us that they had felt the same as we did when they first arrived at the clinic; wondering what the hell they were doing in Tijuana to get well. They, too, had gone through the traditional medical treatments. They had chemotherapy and radiation, and finally, after all their pain and suffering they had been told that there was no hope: "Sorry, we are unable to do anything more; you only have a few months left to live."

I sat quietly, looking out the window and contemplating these amazing stories. I began mulling over the events I'd experienced with Mom since Christmas. I reflected on how much a person's perception and understanding drastically changes when one is faced with death or the death of a loved one. Mom had been given a death sentence by traditional doctors and because of that it had forced all of us to be open minded. What we had thought was ridiculous suddenly seemed plausible; because traditional medicine had nothing to offer us, and we had no hope, we began to look at alternative medicine much differently. This was a whole new world for us, and it was a big eye opener on every level.

I thought about the patients visiting the clinic that day. They were no different than us. They were just further down the path of self-healing than we were. Talking to these brave people inspired confidence that the doctors in this clinic would be able to help Mom as well.

I turned from the window and put my attention on Mom. I could see that she was tired. It was late afternoon, and the doctor still hadn't called her back into his office for her second and last visit. Looking around, I noticed that the waiting room was almost empty. Many of the patients had left for the day to go back home. I wished that we were leaving too.

I felt sorry for Mom; she was still recuperating from her operation, and sitting all day had exhausted her.

She was finally called in at 5:30 p.m. to see the doctor, and this time Mom asked me come into the office with her. My first impression of the doctor was that he seemed to be a very warm and compassionate man.

He began, "Upon studying the x-rays, I feel there is still hope for you. There is no reason why you can't fight this particular cancer. Many patients have been much worse than you, and they are alive and well today."

Mom looked excited and said, "It's good to know that I can go home and fight this. At least I can try something."

The doctor agreed, "Yes, you can. Many patients come to this clinic with no hope at all. This is not right. People should always have hope and keep trying."

He then made out a prescription for the many items Mom had to buy at the clinic's pharmacy. A brief list was calcium, vitamin C, a clinic herbal formula, and shark's cartilage. She was also given a strict diet that was imperative to follow.

As we were leaving, the doctor said, "Please call me if you are having any problems at all."

We left the doctor's office to find Mrs. Rodden waiting in the van to take us to the pharmacy. When we arrived, we stood in line behind a few patients who were picking up their prescriptions. While we were waiting our turn, a lady standing in front of us mentioned that we should buy the shark cartilage from the clinic. She had priced it in Texas, and it was two hundred dollars for the same amount and brand; whereas, at this pharmacy it was only a hundred dollars so we decided to take her advice.

Mom bought three bottles of shark cartilage, the clinic's formula, vitamins, and a cookbook. I was surprised at how inexpensive the bill was for the medicine, the doctor's visit, blood tests, and x-rays. It was less than nine hundred dollars. We were very relieved. We had heard that many of the alternative clinics in Mexico charged extremely high rates of five to twenty-five thousand dollars or more. This was one of the things that had worried us the most.

Driving from the clinic back to our hotel, Mom was excited; she now had an opportunity to possibly beat this cancer.

She said, "The stories that the patients told us today really gave me hope; they sound like miracles, and now maybe a miracle can happen for me too."

☙❧

Exhausted, we arrived at our hotel.

Mom said, "I'm not going to join you guys for dinner, but you go and have a good time. I just want to crawl into a nice cool bed; I'm completely worn out."

Vern and I made sure Mom was comfortable, and then we went to the hotel lounge and ordered dinner and a glass of wine. While we were waiting for our drinks, we discussed our thoughts about the clinic.

"I have to say, I'm impressed by the number of people we met today who are in remission after following the clinic's protocol," said Vern.

"Yes, it's hard to believe. I am so glad you came on this trip with us, because explaining what we experienced today at this clinic would have been impossible."

"I don't think I would have believed you if I hadn't seen it with my own eyes. I feel very positive about this clinic. After what I saw today, if I ever got cancer, I would come here first, before I tried other forms of cancer treatments," said Vern.

"I think I would too," I agreed. "I would at least give it a try, and if it didn't work I would then turn to traditional medicine."

We enjoyed our meal and conversation. It had been a long, hard day, so we decided to call it an early night.

ॐ॰ॐ

The next afternoon, my friends Howard and Debbie from San Diego offered to take us sightseeing to many of the popular tourist attractions in the area. Mom was in good spirits and somehow mustered up an incredible amount of energy; she was very keen to see as much as possible.

The last three days of our trip were very enjoyable. We sat around the pool during the day, and in the evening we went to charming restaurants on the harbor front for dinner. It was the first time in over twenty-five years that the three of us had been together without our spouses or our children. In this short time together, we formed a strong bond that I knew would never be broken. It had been a very successful trip.

On the fifth day, we boarded the plane mid-morning to head back to Canada. Once we had settled ourselves in our seats, Mom said, "I'm really excited to get back home and start my new diet. I now have some tools to fight this cancer. I now have hope."

"I'm glad you feel that this trip was worthwhile, Mom. I feel hopeful too."

I sat back in my seat and thought about how glad I was that we had experienced this clinic. It had helped Mom form an optimistic, positive outlook regarding getting well again. The doctor at the clinic was right. We should never give up; there is always hope.

We arrived in Vancouver on June 3. Vern said goodbye to us at the terminal. He boarded a plane to Victoria, and we boarded the evening plane to Vernon.

We landed at the Vernon Airport at 8:00 p.m. that evening. As we walked through the arrival doors, we were immediately greeted by Corky and the kids. The kids raced up to us and gave us loads of hugs and kisses.

The kids said to Mom, "Hi Grandma we missed you! Did you get us anything?"

I gave the kids the 'evil eye' and told them that they shouldn't ask questions like that. But Mom couldn't help herself. She laughed and said, "Of course I did. You'll see soon."

I told them that they would have to wait until they got home to get their gifts. They reluctantly conceded, and we went to the baggage claim area to pick up our luggage.

Mom had acquired the nickname of "Grandma Claus" over the years. Whenever she came to visit us, she would always come with bags filled with gifts for everyone; the kids knew without a doubt that their Grandma had bought them something this time, too.

On the twenty-five minute drive to Mom's house, we told Corky what we had experienced at the clinic.

He said, "I'm so glad the trip to Mexico has turned out to be such a success. It sounds so positive, Anne."

"Well, it was a very encouraging experience. The doctor was fantastic and the people we met had such good results with the medicine, so I'm going to give it a good shot and see what happens for me. If they can do it, why can't I?"

"I like your attitude, Anne. You're absolutely right, why wouldn't it happen for you too."

When we arrived at Mom's house, she gave the kids and Corky their presents. We made sure that she had everything she needed for the night, and then we headed home.

I always found it difficult to leave Mom at her house, alone. I had become very protective of her and worried about her being lonely. I had frequently asked her over the years if she wished she could find someone to marry or at least have a companion to share her life with.

She would often say, "Carole, I've been on my own for twenty years. I'm used to my own space, and I don't mind being alone at all. Now saying that, I will admit that there are times when I think it would be nice to date someone on a casual basis, but I don't want to have to take care of them. I did that long enough with your father, and now I really like my freedom and independence."

Chapter 6

It was good to be back home and so nice to be waking up in my own bed. One of the first thoughts that came to mind was, "Now we have something that Mom can do to actively fight this cancer".

I got out of bed and woke the kids for school. As I was making their breakfast, Tess asked, "Mom is Grandma going to get better now?"

I said, "She's sure trying to get better. She has medicine from the clinic in Mexico, and we hope it'll work."

She said, "I hope so too, 'cause I'm tired of Grandma being sick."

I stopped what I was doing and wondered what she had meant by that. Had I been so pre-occupied with Mom and her problems that I hadn't spent enough time with my daughter? At that moment, I painfully recognized that I had been neglecting the kids on an emotional level.

I went over to Tess, held her hand, and gently said, "I know this has been really hard on you. I know I haven't been here as much as usual, and I appreciate how understanding you have been. I'm really sorry, but Grandma has needed my help a lot lately. There isn't anyone else for her to turn to."

Tess got up from the table, put on her coat and said, "I know Mom, but I'm still really tired of it."

I gave her a hug, and we didn't say anything more about it. This was one of the first times—and one of many to come—that the kids let me know they were upset with me. I was torn between my family and my mother. I thought that because the kids' lives were stable and secure they could spare some of my time as I had always been a full time Mom. Obviously, I was wrong.

After the kids left for school, I pondered what Tess had said. I wondered if the kids were affected by my impatience more than my absence. I seemed to be more irritable than usual and tears were often close to the surface. The truth was I was just darn right exhausted. I could see that Tess was not sick of Grandma being sick;

she was upset that I was gone so much and that I wasn't my available, patient self.

I made a mental note to try and be more engaged and tolerant. I was coping with a terminally ill person, and it had crept into every part of my life; everything and everyone was being affected to one degree or another.

I cleaned up the kitchen dishes, and once I was finished, I phoned Mom to ask her how she was feeling.

"Oh Carole, it was sure nice to be in my own bed again. I'm sure happy to be home, but I noticed this morning that I don't have much to eat."

"That was one of the reasons I called you. I wanted to ask you if there's anything I can do for you today or if there's anything that you might need."

"Well, I need groceries. I do hate to bother you, but could you take me shopping this morning? I have very little food in the house that I can eat on my new diet."

"Sure. I just have to tidy the house a bit and then I'll be right over."

Mom was ready to go shopping when I arrived at her house; she got into the van and said, "I hope I can get most of the groceries that I need from the natural food store."

I said, "Well, let's go and see what we can find. I'm sure they will have most of the items that are on your list."

Mom could not eat foods with preservatives or additives. She wasn't allowed any sugar or any refined foods at all. Fruits and vegetables had to be fresh and organic. She could not eat any canned or frozen foods because they were loaded with preservatives. Mom was used to the regular North American diet, so this was going to take a lot of effort on her part to follow through with this new way of eating.

We stocked Mom's house with fresh organic vegetables, meats, and dairy, and I got to take all her canned and frozen foods home. Somehow, I didn't feel so good about that. I wasn't sure I wanted to eat them, either. I decided then that we all needed to change our eating habits.

It was inspiring to see her so determined and certain that she was going to beat the odds. For the next two-and-a-half weeks, Mom was faithful to her diet and followed the prescribed medicine to the letter, but out of the blue, she began to vomit after meals.

She went to see the doctor and asked him what could be causing her to be sick. Unfortunately, he didn't have any answers to this problem. His only suggestion was to take an over-the-counter anti-nausea drug before meals to help keep the food down. Mom took the pills as prescribed, but the problem persisted.

Mom had been ingesting the medicine from the clinic for close to three weeks when she decided that it was the shark cartilage that was upsetting her stomach. The powder was very fishy-tasting and made her feel unwell, so she began taking it in capsule form. This seemed to work for a week, but to her disappointment, she started getting sick again. She was sure that it was the shark cartilage, but she didn't want to quit taking it because it was an important ingredient for decreasing the size of the cancerous tumor.

So Mom decided to phone the doctor in Mexico to talk to him about the problem she was having. He suggested cutting the dose in half to see if she could tolerate a smaller amount. After speaking to the doctor, she waited another week before adding the shark cartilage back in her diet, but unfortunately she continued to be sick in the meantime. She began thinking that maybe it was the herbal formula that was making her ill. Finally she stopped taking everything the clinic had prescribed, but to her dismay, this did not stop the stomach problems. We were beginning to surmise that there was something else going on.

෨෧

Early in July, Mom phoned me in a panic and in excruciating pain. "Can you take me to the hospital? My bowel is completely blocked."

This was the first bowel blockage she'd had since before her operation.

She said, "My bag has been empty all day, and I have terrible stomach pains. I don't know what's wrong."

"Mom, I'll be right there! Just hang tight."

I rushed over to her house to find her sitting on the couch, slumped over in agony. She had a bucket beside her in case she got sick.

She admitted, "I've been like this all day."

"What! Why didn't you phone me sooner? Let's get you to the hospital right now."

I helped her into the van and rushed her to the Emergency Unit. The nurse immediately administered pain medication and admitted Mom into the hospital. She was in so much pain that the nurse had to give her another injection of pain medication. She told Mom that she could only ingest clear fluids until her bowel released. This would relax the bowel and get it working smoothly again.

Once Mom's pain had subsided, an orderly arrived and wheeled Mom's bed to the ward on the second floor for the night. I stayed with her until she was comfortable and pain-free. When I left her hospital room, she was sleeping peacefully.

అలఉ

The next morning, I arrived at the hospital to find that Mom had improved. The nurse at the desk told me that her bowel had finally released in the night.

I walked into Mom's room and said, "You're looking relaxed. I see you are feeling better."

"Yes," she said with a smile. "My bag is finally filling up again, and the pain is all gone."

"Thank heavens for that," I said. "You were in a lot of pain yesterday. Did the doctor tell you why this happened?"

"Well, they think it was the corn on the cob that I ate for dinner a couple of nights ago. Apparently, with a colostomy certain foods can block the passage, so I guess I can't have it anymore. I love it so much, but I don't want to feel like that again."

"I guess not. Did they give you any other suggestions?"

"Yes, I shouldn't eat anything with skin, like peas or tomatoes."

"Well, you learned something here. It's too bad they didn't tell you this before."

"Yes, I said the exact same thing to them too, but the nurse told me that it's a hit-or-miss sort of thing. Some people can eat everything, and it doesn't bother them at all."

She changed the subject and said, "But more importantly, can you get me out of here? I want to leave the hospital right away if I can."

"Are you sure you're ready?"

"Hell, yes!"

We both began laughing just as the nurse walked in.

She asked, "What's so funny?"

"Mom wants to get out of the hospital as fast as she can."

She said, "I don't blame you. I'd feel the same way. Your timing is perfect. I was just coming to tell you the doctor left orders that whenever you feel better, you can go home."

"Great, I'll get dressed right now!"

I left the hospital with Mom less than twenty minutes later.

We drove into Mom's driveway, just in time to meet the home care nurse. We told her what had transpired the day before with the bowel blockage and the hospital stay. She agreed that corn could easily have been one of the culprits that caused her bowel blockage.

Mom said, "I feel good now. I'm so glad we discovered what the problem was. I'm going to have to watch my diet very closely and not eat too much roughage. Obviously this blockage and my stomach upset aren't caused by the shark cartilage or the clinic's formula, so I'm going to start taking them again and give it a good try."

I had to leave Mom's house to pick the kids up from school. As I drove out of her driveway, I intuitively felt that there was something much greater than corn blocking Mom's bowel. I had a sense that the cancer was getting worse and was blocking the passage. I think the doctor knew this too but didn't want to come out and say it.

Chapter 7

July had its ups and downs. The good news was that Mom began driving her car at the beginning of the month. This was giving her the freedom to do whatever she wanted, and it was encouraging seeing her out and about, leading a somewhat normal life. But as the month progressed, she began having more frequent bowel obstructions. She phoned me on many occasions in July, saying that her bag was empty and she was in intense pain. I would take her to the hospital, and the doctor would admit her until the bowel released—usually by the next day. On top of the bowel blockages, she was throwing up on a regular basis.

She'd say, "It must be the cream soups. I won't eat those anymore," or "Salads seem to be too hard to digest, so I'll avoid them."

She was always trying to find the right food that would stay in her stomach.

By the third week of July, Mom had been admitted to the hospital eight times. The doctor felt it was time to put her name on the palliative care list and designated her as a terminally ill patient. This gave her the freedom to bypass the waiting room in the Emergency Unit and get immediate medical attention for relief of pain and symptoms. I felt this was a positive step for Mom, but she felt the opposite and was very offended by this new turn of events.

She said, "It's as if I'm supposed to give up and die. I phone my doctor when I'm in pain, and he tells me to go to the Emergency Room. But the times I've been admitted, he didn't even come visit me on his morning rounds. It's as if I'm already dead."

I tried to comfort her, "Mom, he just wants you to have the privilege of not having to sit in the waiting room for hours before anyone gets a chance to see you. If your name is registered, you can go straight to a bed and have medical care immediately."

She felt that by accepting this service, she was submitting to the cancer she had. After some discussion, she realized that it was in her best interests to go on the list, and so she finally conceded.

 споро

At the end of July, I rushed Mom to the Emergency Room with another bowel obstruction and the worst pain she had felt in months.

On this particular day, a handsome, young, Welsh doctor named Dr. Morgan happened to be on call. I immediately sensed that there was something special about him; he was very caring and sincerely concerned for Mom. After completing a thorough examination, he wrote a prescription to help her with indigestion and gas. This was the first time in over a month that a doctor had suggested a different medication to ease her discomfort. As usual, Mom was admitted into the hospital for an overnight stay until her bowel released.

I left the hospital once Mom was pain free and settled for the night. Walking to my van, I thought about what a difficult month this had been and how emotionally and physically exhausted I was. As I drove out of the parking lot, my emotions got the best of me and I burst into tears. I just couldn't understand why this was happening to Mom. Why did she have to go through all this pain and suffering?

I wasn't in the mood to go home, so instead I drove down a country road and parked at a lookout with a view the city. Gazing at the lights, I began to swear at God. I yelled in frustration and immense anger. I sobbed as my pain and sorrow poured out of me until there was nothing left but deep sadness. The full impact of Mom's illness was sinking in.

The medical community avoided talking to me about Mom's progressing illness. No one wanted to tell us what the future had in store, yet it was so obvious that they knew exactly what was going to happen.

The realization of how brutal cancer can be was becoming crystal clear. It was obvious that there was going to be more pain and anguish to deal with before this was over. I just knew it. But how long was I going to be able to handle this constant emotional turmoil?

My life had come to a grinding halt. I was constantly at the beck and call of my mother and her illness.

Through red, puffy eyes, I looked at the clock and noticed it was after eleven; I needed to get home. By the time I entered my garage, I was completely drained. I unlocked the door and was relieved to find that everyone asleep. Given how I felt, I wasn't up to facing anyone. Corky was getting used to me coming and going at all hours of the night; he knew I was either at the hospital or at Mom's house.

As I quietly tip-toed upstairs, I thought how my husband never complained that I wasn't home a lot or that meals weren't made. I had been trying not to burden him with my pain. He had enough on his plate with his business and with the extra load of the kids.

I dragged myself to bed and wondered what was going to happen next. If I knew then what I know now, I think I would have completely fallen to pieces.

I drove to the hospital around eight-thirty the next morning to find Mom sitting up in her bed, drinking juice.

The first thing she said to me as I walked into the room was, "Dr. Morgan was in to see me. He said that I can leave the hospital anytime, so I'd like to get ready and go."

"Okay, Mom. I'll get your clothes, and you can change."

She continued, "I've decided that he's going to be my doctor now. He's done more for me in twenty-four hours than my other doctor did in three months."

Listening to Mom brought back a recent article I had read stating that a big part of the healing process was having a kind, compassionate doctor; one that you could trust. Dr. Morgan certainly seemed to have these qualities, and if she liked him, then I was happy.

ॐ−ॐ

We were into the month of August, and school holidays were more than half over. The kids and I needed a change of scenery, so I planned a holiday at Beaver Foot Lodge: a horse ranch in the Rocky

Mountains. I didn't want to leave Mom alone, so my sister-in-law Sandy offered to come and spend time with her while I was gone.

This was a much needed break for me and the kids. Riding horses up in the Rocky Mountains with my friend Jennifer and her kids was just the medicine I needed. It was a very relaxing, fun time. I realized how important it was to get away from all the stress that I had been under for the last seven months, and I vowed to keep my good spirits when I got back. But after four restful days, I arrived home to find out that Mom had been admitted for an overnight stay at the hospital for yet another bowel obstruction. The very day I arrived home, Mom dropped a bomb shell on me.

She said, "I want to go back to Tijuana for my three-month check-up."

I thought, Oh no, I can't do this again, this is crazy! She was in pain a lot of the time now, the blockages were becoming more complicated and frequent, and, on top of it all, she was losing weight rapidly.

I really wanted to dissuade her against taking this trip, so with a lot of apprehension, I said, "You know that you won't get any medical insurance, and lately you have been having a lot of bowel obstructions. Do you think this is a good idea?"

"Yes I do. Maybe they can do something for me. Maybe they can give me some new ideas on how to take this medicine without getting sick. I haven't kept down even a quarter of what I need to take to beat this cancer. I have to go."

It was true; the clinic's medicine wasn't much use to her in the state she was in. She wasn't getting enough in her system to shrink the tumor. I remembered back to last month's check-up with the surgeon. He had asked Mom if she was trying any alternative medicine. Mom and I had sheepishly looked at each other and finally she admitted that she was.

The surgeon had said, "The tumor is definitely smaller, so whatever you're taking seems to be helping. Keep doing whatever you are doing."

We were so excited! It was working! But now seeing Mom like

this, I was deflated. There had to be a way to take the medicine and keep it down.

I mulled over the idea of another trip to Mexico. Mom was definitely too weak and frail to be going to Mexico again, but she hadn't been able to take the medicine from the clinic for almost five weeks and she was desperate. I wasn't comfortable going on this trip; for that matter, the thought scared me half to death. But how could I deny her another opportunity to get well? It was her only hope, and who was I to take that away from her?

So I took a deep breath and said, "Well Mom, we must be nuts, but we'll go. Let's hope we get through this without any major complications. I'll make the flight arrangements. I really hope you don't get a bowel blockage when we're down there. The clinic isn't a hospital, and they can't keep you over night."

"If I get another blockage, then I'll get on a plane right away and get back to Canada." With confidence and a smile she added, "Don't worry, we will be okay."

I, on the other hand, had no confidence about this whatsoever. I wondered what the family would say about this crazy trip that we were about to embark on.

๖•๙

I booked our flights, hotel, and shuttle service to the clinic for the next week. As I had anticipated, I was unable to get medical coverage for Mom, for anything related to her operation or to cancer.

With everything arranged, I spent the next week agonizing over the trip. Mom's health was definitely declining; she was losing weight rapidly and had become noticeably frail. She had been five feet, one inch tall before her illness, but now she appeared so much shorter than that.

I was certain at this point that I had, without any doubt at all, lost my mind to be taking her to Mexico in this condition.

Corky drove us to the airport to catch our flight to San Diego. Mom was hopeful and excited about going back to the clinic, but I was on edge. I was not excited at all. I was dreading this trip, and I just hoped that we would get through it without any disasters. I really wished my brother could have come with us, but it was impossible for him to take any extra time off work.

Corky knew I was distressed and tried to assure me that everything would be all right while we were in the States. He said if worst came to worst, we could just fly back to Canada. But I knew Corky well enough to know, that even though he was being supportive, he was anxious about this insane trip we were about to embark on.

So with great trepidation, Mom and I boarded the plane to Vancouver. We changed planes in Seattle, and then we sat back and relaxed for the three hour flight to San Diego. Shortly after takeoff, I glanced over at Mom and noticed that she had her eyes closed with a slight grimace on her face.

I leaned over and asked, "Are you okay Mom?"

She said, "I have a few cramps, but I'm fine, really, so don't worry."

Don't worry? I responded in my head, you have cramps and we've hardly left the airport! I wondered how we were going to manage four nights away from the hospital. We seriously had to be out of our minds to be going to the United States with no health insurance for Mom.

We arrived in San Diego late in the afternoon without any mishaps and caught a taxi to our hotel. Mom had wanted to stay at a less expensive hotel this time because she felt it was a waste of money. The hotel lobby was nice enough, but when we walked into our room we were disappointed. The carpets were soiled and the wallpaper was old and drab. I was immediately annoyed with my travel agent. She had assured me it was a lovely hotel situated close to the water, but she had failed to mention that it was miles from the downtown core of the city.

I would figure out this problem with the hotel later, the most important thing I had to do at this time was to phone Mrs. Rodden to confirm our pick up time for the next morning. Once that was settled, I relaxed and began unpacking my suitcase. As I was hanging up my clothes, I brought up a past conversation about Mom taking a trip to England.

She said, "You know, I think about going on a trip like that all the time. I should have retired five years ago. I was stupid to have thought that I didn't have enough money. Now what good is all that money in the bank?"

"Exactly, Mom. I know San Diego wouldn't be the first pick if you were well, but let's make this trip as good as we can." I went on, "Mom, I am really sorry about the poor job I did picking this hotel. We can move to a nicer place if you want. The hotel we stayed at last time was in a better location and much nicer than this one."

Mom said, "Yes, I loved that it was situated on the boardwalk. I really enjoy the walks along the seafront. The area was so alive with lots of people. There was so much to see and do. But let's think about moving later. My main concern right now is getting to the clinic."

Mom was tired from the long trip and didn't want to do much, so I went for a short walk by myself and bought a sandwich for dinner, to eat along the way. I arrived back at our hotel room an hour later and found Mom ready for bed.

I said, "It's been a long day for you, you must be really exhausted."

"Yes," Mom sighed. "It sure has been a long day. I think I'll go to sleep now. I'm exhausted."

We awoke at 6:30 the next morning to be sure to get to the clinic before nine. Mom had high hopes that the doctor would find a solution to her bowel problem that would put her back on the road to recovery.

Mrs. Rodden arrived at the hotel at 8:00 am to drive us to the clinic. We crossed the border with ease: just a few questions and then we were on the road again, arriving at the clinic around 8:30. This assured Mom's acceptance as a patient that day.

It was strange to be back; it was as if we had just been there a few days earlier. Everything looked the same except for the patients in the waiting room. I didn't recognize anyone from our first visit in June.

As I looked around the clinic, I began calculating: If there were twenty-five or so patients coming daily to the clinic, how many was that a month, or a year? It was shocking to think that there were so many people with cancer desperately seeking help.

Mom walked out of the changing area dressed in a blue gown. She handed the nurse her urine sample and disappeared into a room for blood tests. She knew the routine this time and didn't feel out of place or as nervous as she had been on her first visit.

Finally, when all the tests were completed, Mom sat down beside me and said, "Well I guess we're going to be sitting here all day again. I just spoke with the receptionist, and she said that it was busy, but not as bad as some days."

We prepared ourselves for the fact that we would be hanging around in the waiting room for hours to come. This wasn't easy for Mom. She wasn't feeling well, her bowel had not moved for two days, and she was having painful cramps; but, as usual, she said that she was fine. All that mattered to her was having the opportunity to see the doctor, and, hopefully, he would have a solution for dissolving the tumor.

I stayed in the waiting room while Mom went for x-rays. As I watched Mom walk away with the nurse, I noticed a pretty young woman sitting beside her husband with a small child. She gave me a warm smile. I smiled back and decided that I would strike up a conversation by asking where they were from. The wife said that they were from Saskatchewan and that she had recently been diagnosed with terminal cancer. This was her first visit to the clinic.

As we continued talking, she began telling me a little about herself. She and her husband were born and raised as Hutterites and were part of a religious community. Her husband was a farmer, and, from what I gathered, they worked very hard and lived a very simple existence. She had recently been told by her family doctor back home to get her affairs in order, that she had very little time to live. She was crushed at being diagnosed as terminally ill. She had come to the clinic on a recommendation by a member of her church who was in remission because of the treatment given by the clinic. She had great faith that she was going to be well again.

A lady sitting beside me interrupted our conversation and asked if she could tell her story as it might put some of our fears to rest about the clinic. She had brought her five-year-old daughter for her second visit to the clinic because she had an inoperable brain tumor.

She began her story, "A year ago, my daughter was diagnosed with a brain tumor. The doctor insisted that she should have radiation and chemotherapy immediately to shrink the tumor. At that time, I told the doctor that I wanted to try less drastic measures. I wanted to try alternative treatments first because I was really worried about the toxicity of traditional cancer treatments. The doctor was furious with me. He took out a court order to stop me, and to my horror, he won. The court agreed that she should have chemotherapy and radiation. I had no choice but to follow through with the judge's ruling. If I didn't do what they said, they would take her away from me and put her in a foster home while they performed these treatments."

I was absolutely stunned by what she was telling me. I asked, "How did you and your daughter handle all of this?"

She said, "The chemotherapy and radiation almost killed her. The doctors gave both of these toxic treatments at the same time because they felt they had to be aggressive. The outcome of the treatment was that the tumor actually grew bigger. Finally, I'd had it. I told the doctor that I was going to take her to Mexico, and again he disagreed and said he wanted to operate."

She continued, "By this time, I was enraged. They had already told me that it was too dangerous to operate and that it could severely damage her mentally. I adamantly refused to allow them to do this. So again, the doctor took out another court order against me.

"Thank God the judge said that it was not the right of the court to okay this procedure because it was so dangerous. He said it was the parent's choice. So the long and the short of it is that we are in Mexico again, for the second time. My daughter has been taking the prescribed medicine from this clinic for the last three months, and the tumor has shrunk to less than half the size that it was."

I said, "I can't even imagine what you have been through."

At that moment, the nurse came over to us and told the mother and little girl that they could leave the clinic because the visit was over. The little girl slid off her chair and began jumping up and down in glee. She was so happy to get out of there, and her exuberance was contagious. We all began laughing. She was so cute.

Her mom told us that her daughter had been in a lot of pain with the chemotherapy and she had been poked and prodded so much by doctors that to her, all doctors were scary.

I said, "Good luck and thank you for sharing your story. It really gives me hope for my mom."

Looking around the room, I saw many faces filled with hope. These people were not ready to die. They were fighting for their lives, trying to gain more time. They were determined to do everything they could to live. I was truly inspired by the fact that they would not accept their doctors' prognoses and were doing everything they could to heal themselves. They were not giving up.

I looked at my watch and wondered why Mom was taking so long for just a few x-rays. Finally, an hour later, she arrived back in the waiting room and sat down on a chair beside me.

I asked, "What took you so long?"

"The clinic's x-ray machine broke down, so they had to take us to the hospital in town to get the x-rays done."

"Do you mean you actually went into the city in your gown? You didn't put your clothes on?"

Mom laughed and said, "I never thought the day would come that I would go out in public in a hospital gown with my knee high nylons rolled down around my ankles!"

We both howled with laughter. Thank God Mom still had a good sense of humor.

A few minutes later it was Mom's turn to go into the doctor's office. Once Mom was on the examination table, the doctor performed a complete physical exam. Mom had weighed approximately one hundred and twenty pounds for most of her adult life, but now I could see that she was much less than that. She couldn't have weighed more than ninety-five pounds. There was very little flesh on her legs, there was no muscle tone, and the skin hung in folds. It made me want to cry to see her so thin.

The doctor said that he had studied the x-rays, and he could see that she had formed another blockage in her small intestine. He asked if Mom's doctor in Vernon was aware of this.

Mom said, "Well they think that's what I have, but they haven't done an x-ray in the last three months. I've asked the doctor to do something, maybe even operate again, but they said that it would be too risky because I was so thin, I could bleed to death."

He said grimly, "If you don't get an operation, Anne, you are going to die. The obstruction will stop you from getting any nutrition and hinder you from absorbing the medicine I have prescribed."

Mom desperately replied, "I would be willing to have an operation, but they won't do it."

"Then you have to find a different doctor who will. Our clinic doesn't do any surgical procedures here."

He went on to say, "In the meantime, because you are having trouble keeping the medicine in your stomach, I want you to try something different. Put three teaspoonfuls of shark cartilage in water to make a paste, then put it in a syringe and insert it into your rectum. The many scientific studies done in Europe used the shark cartilage this way. This procedure was found to be very effective; it will be absorbed quickly into your system."

He continued, "Upon comparing your x-rays from June and those taken today, I can see the tumor has shrunk. This is a good sign, even though you haven't taken the medicine consistently. I feel if you can unblock the bowel, you will have the chance you need to fight this cancer."

At this point Mom looked really disheartened, but she didn't say anything. She just sat with her hands folded in her lap and listened intently.

He said, "Here is a prescription for more of the clinic's formula. This is a little different from what you have been using before. I want you to double the dosage." He stood up and said, "I hope you can get help back home, and if you have any questions at all, please call me."

We were free to leave the clinic. We found Mrs. Rodden in the waiting area, ready to take us to the pharmacy.

Once we were settled in the car, I said, "So Mom, what do you think?"

"Well, I guess I wanted to hear better news than this. How am I going to get an operation when I weigh so little?"

"When we get back home, you can ask Dr. Morgan if he knows a surgeon who would operate. Hopefully, he'll have some answers for you."

Mom was discouraged. The thought of going through another operation was daunting, but it seemed that the bigger challenge now was finding a surgeon who would do it.

We picked up the medicine and headed back to San Diego.

I found myself thinking about the people back home who were worried about us going to Mexico to find help for Mom. I was so glad that we had taken the chance; we were so lucky to have found this remarkable clinic. The doctors and support staff were without a doubt dedicated to giving patients the opportunity to get back to good health in a non-toxic way. I witnessed people who never gave up and who won the battle; I saw that there is always hope.

We arrived back at our hotel much earlier than we had anticipated. This was a huge relief because Mom's cramps were much stronger than they were when she woke up that morning, and on top of it all, she was exhausted.

We said goodbye to Mrs. Rodden and went straight to our room. Mom immediately got into bed and closed her eyes to rest. I could see she was in pain.

I anxiously suggested, "Maybe I should phone the airline and get you on a plane and back to Canada as soon as possible. It will cost you a few hundred dollars more, but at least you would be home, close to Dr. Morgan. I'll stay here and fly back on my scheduled ticket."

Mom agreed, "Maybe you're right, I think I should go home. The cramps are coming on so strong now."

I called the airline to book a seat for Mom on a flight that evening. Her ticket was non-refundable, so it would cost another thousand dollars for the flight back to Vancouver. Unfortunately, there wasn't a connecting flight to Vernon until tomorrow and that would mean she would have to stay in a hotel by herself in Vancouver over night.

She admitted, "I don't know what to do. It could release at any moment and then I'd be fine, or it could last another day or two."

I tried to reassure her that at least she would be on Canadian soil and could go to the hospital in Vancouver if she needed to.

Mom said hesitantly, "I feel nervous about going back to Vancouver by myself, feeling like this."

"That's not a problem. Forget about the money, Mom. We can go together."

By this time, she was getting razor-sharp pains. Just as I was giving Mom a glass of water and a couple of painkillers, there was a knock on the door.

I wondered who it could be, and then I remembered that we had invited Debbie, my friend from San Diego, to come by for dinner. I should have cancelled, but what with Mom being in so much pain and me phoning the airlines, I completely forgot.

I answered the door and Debbie came in the room. She was distressed to see Mom so sick and so thin compared to our last visit three months earlier.

I expressed our dilemma, "Debbie, we're trying to figure out what we should do. Mom's in a lot of pain, and we don't know whether or not to stay in San Diego."

Debbie offered, "I can drive you both to the airport if you decide to go home."

Mom interrupted, "Listen, you guys go for dinner. I will be alright for half an hour. I'll rest here and think about what we should do."

"Okay, we won't be long. We'll be downstairs in the restaurant if you need us for anything at all."

We rushed through our meal and arrived back in the room within the hour to find Mom feeling a bit better.

She said, "I don't feel as bad as I did. The painkillers have taken the edge off some of the pain. Let's see how I feel tomorrow; we can make a decision then. I'm just too tired to think about it this evening."

I said apprehensively, "If you're sure Mom. I do feel extremely nervous about being in the States with your bowel being blocked, but I'll trust your judgment. We'll talk about it again in the morning."

Chapter 8

The next morning, Mom and I discussed whether or not to book a flight back to Canada as soon as possible. Mom didn't want to leave and made the decision to persevere and stay in San Diego for a few more days. She had a feeling that her bowel was going to work again, and she'd be fine. I, myself, felt very uneasy about the whole thing. I would have liked to have seen her on the plane the night before.

Debbie came to visit around three-thirty that afternoon and asked Mom if she was feeling up to going out. If so, she would take us sightseeing.

Mom said, "Thank you Debbie, but no. I don't think I'm in any condition to go anywhere right now. When this thing releases, there's going to be quite a flow, and I don't want to be in public when it happens. Why don't you guys go out for awhile? I'm just going to rest and hope this damn thing releases soon."

"No Mom, we'll stay with you, and we can have tea and a visit here. I don't want you to be by yourself feeling the way you do."

"Carole, I'll be alright. This has happened so many times before. I'm sure it will release soon. And to be honest, I really would like to be alone and rest for a few hours. I will be fine, don't worry."

Reluctantly, I said, "Okay, I'll just go out for an hour. I'll call you on a regular basis to check on you. Call me for anything at all; I won't be far from the hotel."

During the drive into town, I expressed my concerns to Debbie and said, "I think Mom and I should fly back to Canada right away, but Mom doesn't want to leave yet. I don't know why she wants to stay. After all, the way it stands now, she can't do anything but sit in her hotel room anyway. And speaking of hotel rooms, I feel badly that I booked that one. I hate to think of her sitting in a grungy, dark room."

Debbie said, "Man, this is tough for you guys. Your mom is so sweet. I feel so bad for her. I can't even comprehend what your mom must be going through."

"I know. She is really amazing; she's so positive. I think I would have given up a long time ago, if I were her."

Debbie said, "Well then, if she's so determined to stay for a few more days, let's see if we can find a better hotel."

"Well, if we do stay for a few more days, I think we should move to a nicer place. I would like to make this trip as enjoyable as possible for her."

Debbie agreed, "I totally get what you're saying. I know of a nice hotel in the same area you stayed last time; let's drive over and check it out, and if she is feeling better, we'll move her."

"Okay, that sounds good."

Once we were on the freeway, I said, "You know Debbie, I am starting to accept that Mom doesn't have long to live. I am not so sure that she is going to beat this cancer. My intuition is telling me that this will be the last time we'll have a holiday together. But that's not something I would ever say to Mom. I would never want to discourage her or take away her will to fight. But how much more can she endure?"

Debbie said, "I can't imagine suffering the way your mother has."

❧❦

We drove to the hotel on the beach. The hotel was as lovely as Debbie had described. It had a beautiful pool with a large waterfall and plenty of comfortable, padded, reclining chairs placed throughout the courtyard.

"This is perfect," I said. "If Mom's too tired to do any sightseeing, she can at least sit by the water and enjoy the day."

We walked to the front desk, and as luck would have it, they had a standard room available. The rate wasn't much more than the hotel we were staying at, I decided to pay the difference so that Mom wouldn't worry about the cost.

I phoned Mom to see how things were going and to tell her about the hotel. She answered the phone in a panic, "Carole, thank God you've phoned! I'm in desperate need of some flanges and bags. My bowel has released, and it's running out of me like water and I don't have any bags left. I've been phoning around to different pharmacies, but none of them have my flange and bag size."

"What! Why didn't you phone me before now?" I quickly turned to Debbie and asked her where we could find medical supplies. She suggested that the mall had a large pharmacy that would be able to help us.

I asked Mom for the brand, bag, and flange size and promised to get them to her as soon as I could.

With relief Mom said, "Thank you so much, most of the pain has gone. Thank God."

It was almost closing time, so we ran to the car and drove as fast as we could to the mall. We parked and raced through the underground parking lot to the pharmacy. I ran up to the counter and asked the pharmacist if she had half-inch colostomy flanges and bags. She looked behind the counter and said, "Sorry. We're out of that size, but the pharmaceutical store about three miles from here may have them."

I said, "Could you please phone and see if they have any? I'm from out of town, and my mom desperately needs them."

She hesitated. She wasn't particularly friendly, and I could tell that she rarely did this for customers. Begrudgingly, she phoned the other store.

"Well, you're in luck. They have the size you want, but not the brand."

Relieved, I said, "I don't think the brand matters. She'll use anything so long as it works."

She said, "The pharmaceutical store is closing in ten minutes, so you need to hurry."

"Please, "I begged. "Could you ask them to stay open and tell them that we might be a little late, but we'll definitely be there?"

She told the pharmacist we would be there right away. He said that it was not a problem to wait a few extra minutes.

Debbie and I raced to the car. We drove out of the mall parking lot and flew out on to the street. Debbie wasn't sure where the medical supply place was, and I was sure we were going to be too late. Driving like maniacs, taking many wrong turns and wrong streets, we finally arrived at our destination. We ran into the store. We must have looked like a couple of raving lunatics.

The pharmacist looked up from what he was doing to find two crazed women standing at his counter, panting. He broke into laughter and said, "You must be the lady who phoned."

"Yes," I said breathlessly. "Thank you for staying open so late. You don't know how much we appreciate this."

I bought three boxes of colostomy supplies, and with a sigh of relief, we drove as quickly as we could back to the hotel.

We arrived at the hotel room in record time. We found Mom on the bed in a terrible mess.

"Carole, thank God you are here." Exasperated, she said, "This is so humiliating! I hate having this colostomy!"

"I know how frustrating this is for you Mom."

I tried to be positive and said, "The good news is that you feel better and the pain has subsided now that your bowel is working again. Come on, let's get you cleaned up and back in working order."

The first thing we did was get a bag secured into the flange and then Mom went into the shower. I washed her soiled clothes in the sink and hung them outside on the deck to dry.

Mom came out of the bathroom and said, "I can't believe how much better I feel when my bag is filling up again. I am so thankful to you guys, I was really desperate. I don't know what I would have done without you."

As she walked over to the window, she said, "When you were gone, I went for a walk to see if that would help to release my blockage. I sat out front of the hotel and noticed that there isn't anything to do around here; no shops or walking paths. It looks like we'll have to take a taxi everywhere."

I said, "I know. This hotel is really out of the way. I was at another hotel when I called you earlier. It's right next door to the hotel we stayed at last time. If we want to move, it will cost fifty dollars more per night than here, but I think it's more than worth it."

To my complete surprise, she turned to me and said, "You're doing this for yourself, not me. You're so selfish Carole. It's too expensive!"

I was taken aback.

"What are talking about? I was planning on paying the difference. But if it's such a big deal, I'll pay the whole damn thing!"

I took a deep breath. I could feel my anger coming to the surface, "Why are you so worried about money anyway? You can't take it with you, you know!"

At this point, Debbie tactfully left the room and said that she would be in the lobby.

Mom continued, "You just want to go there so you'll have something to do. You left me here by myself today. I sat here with nothing to do while you were out shopping!"

I couldn't believe what she was saying. "Are you kidding me? For your information, I wasn't out shopping. I was out looking for a decent hotel so that you could enjoy your stay here. I left you at four-thirty, and it's now six-thirty. I left because you were adamant that there was no reason for me to hang around because all you felt like doing was resting while you were waiting for your bowel to release."

I couldn't stop; the damn had burst. I took a deep breath and continued, "And how dare you say it is all about me! I have lived and breathed your illness for eight months! I have been at your beck and call twenty-four hours a day. I've been there for you whenever you've needed me, including today. I just spent an hour-and-a-half racing all over San Diego, begging people to help me find colostomy bags for you. I've been running my ass off for you!"

At this point, I knew I had better leave the room before I said more things that I would regret. I was so hurt by what Mom had said. I turned and started walking toward the door when Mom broke down, sobbing. She ran over to me and said, "Oh Carole, I'm so sorry! I'm not myself. I just hate what is happening to me! I'm dying and I can't handle it!"

That was one of the first times Mom ever admitted that she was dying. I put my arm around her while she sobbed. This was the first time I had seen her really break down since she got the news of having cancer.

I said, "Oh, Mom, it's okay. I understand. I was just trying to make these next few days enjoyable for you."

She said, "I know. I love you so much. I didn't mean what I said. You have been the person who has really been there for me. I don't know what I would have done without you."

"Mom, it's alright. The only selfish motive I have is that I want you to enjoy the time you have left."

We hugged each other, and then, wiping her tears, she said, "Let's go to the new hotel; it sounds so much better than here."

I said, "I'll do whatever you want."

That had to be one of the first real fights we'd had since she got sick. It was obvious that Mom had a lot of bottled-up anger and frustration. Up until now, she had put on a brave face to protect us from her pain. It had taken this much suffering and humiliation to finally release some of it, but I knew there was a lot more she wasn't showing me. I knew I had only seen the tip of the iceberg.

I wondered if she would start letting out more of her feelings, but knowing my mother, I doubted it very much. I knew she didn't want to burden me with her sorrow. It bothered me that she wouldn't talk about her pain and sadness. But how do you get someone to talk if they are reluctant to share their deepest feelings?

I gave Mom a hug and then told her that I needed to find Debbie. I went downstairs in the elevator and found her sitting in the lobby. I apologized and invited her back to the room.

Mom said, "I am so sorry Debbie. This has all been very stressful for me. I didn't get very good news from the clinic yesterday, and I guess this was my way of getting it out."

Debbie said that she understood the pressure both of us must be under and not to worry about it at all.

Mom stood up from her chair and said, "Come on, let's pack and move hotels."

We loaded our luggage in Debbie's car and drove to the new hotel.

Walking into the hotel lobby, Mom immediately commented on how beautiful the hotel was. We walked to the front desk and checked in. We took our luggage to our room and then went down to the pool-side and ordered a cool drink. Seeing Mom relaxing made me glad we had moved. This hotel was full of life with lots of people bustling around. It was good for her to be in a lively, upbeat atmosphere.

I leaned back on the hotel lounge chair, closed my eyes, and soaked up the hot sun. My thoughts went to Mom. She had been such an outgoing person and so full of life before she became ill. She had loved to dance and was at her best when entertaining guests. Seeing her now in this weakened state made me sad that those days were over.

That evening, we decided to have dinner in the formal dining room. Once seated at our table, Debbie and I chose the seafood smorgasbord and Mom chose something from the menu because of her strict diet. After the waiter had taken our order, Mom leaned back, relaxed in her chair, and said, "Well, I'm so glad we moved here. It certainly is a lovely hotel, and what I like is that I can wander around and look at the shops on the boardwalk."

Debbie said, "This is a great area; everything is in close walking distance, and there is so much to see and do right outside your hotel. Even sitting on the boardwalk and looking at all the boats is such a nice thing to do."

"Thank you, Debbie, for driving us here. This is such a lovely spot."

We had a great time together, and once we had finished our meal, I asked if anyone was up for a walk along the ocean front.

Debbie said, "I'd love to, but I've got a half-hour drive home and I'm tired." We got up from the table, and Debbie continued, "I'm sorry to say, but I won't be able to come over to see you guys tomorrow, but I'll phone you for sure."

Mom said, "Well Debbie, it's been so nice to have you here with us. Thank you so much for everything you did for me today. I am forever grateful to you."

I could see that Mom was fading; she was exhausted.

She said, "It's getting late, Carole, I really don't feel I can handle a stroll right now. I think I'll go to the room and go straight to bed. It's been a long day and I am beat."

We walked out of the restaurant and into the lobby to say goodbye to Debbie.

I said, "Thank you again for all your help. You saved the day."

As Debbie left, I turned to Mom and said, "I'll come back to the room too. An early night is okay by me."

☙ ❧

The next morning, Mom was feeling quite well, considering the hard time she'd experienced the day before.

I asked, "What would you like to do today? Would you like to go to the mall, or maybe just sit around the pool and rest?"

Mom said, "I wouldn't mind going to the mall. I'd like to buy something for the kids and for Corky."

I smiled and shook my head. As usual, Mom was always thinking of other people.

I ventured to say, "What about you, Mom?" Maybe you could find something nice to wear."

"Oh, I don't really need anything, Carole, but it will be fun to look around though."

I was impressed with her perseverance and willingness to still go out and explore. It amazed me how fast she bounced back after that horrendous ordeal she went through yesterday. I knew if I were in her shoes, I would've had a hard time getting back on my feet. I would have fallen apart for a lot longer than she had.

After breakfast, we took a short taxi ride to the mall. The mall was Southwestern in design, with adobe walls painted a dark pink. It was an outside mall that was very attractive and different from the indoor malls in Canada. As we wandered around, Mom took a few photographs saying she loved the architectural style. She bought sweatshirts for the kids and a T-shirt for Corky.

As we were walking through the courtyard, we came upon a mariachi band playing lively Mexican music. Mom was a bit weary, so she was happy to rest and listen for awhile. I wandered around by myself for about ten minutes and when I got back, I found Mom in a panic.

"Mom, what's wrong?"

"My damn bag has broken again!"

Mom was wearing white slacks and she was terrified that they would get a brown stain for everyone to see. A quick question went through my mind: This has happened so many times; why in the hell does she continue to wear white pants?

I said, "Mom, let's get a taxi and go back to the hotel."

"You don't have to come with me," she insisted. "I'll go and get this fixed up and have a nap. I'm tired, and there's no point in you sitting around the hotel for the rest of the day. I feel fine. I just need to change this damn thing!"

"No, I am coming with you."

We arrived back at the hotel. Mom fixed the bag and sat down on her bed.

She said with annoyance, "This stupid colostomy. The bags never seem to work properly. You would think they would be able to make them leak-free."

I said, "I know it must be frustrating, but there is a good side to them; the colostomy did save your life."

She sighed, "Yes, I suppose so. But what kind of life do I have, living in fear that when I'm out in public, the bag is going to start to leak and smell? I can never really relax when I'm out."

I didn't know what to say. Sometimes I felt so inadequate when it came to trying to console her. In some ways she was right: What kind of life did she have with these bags? Yes, having it did save her life, but it had become her whole life too. It was always on her mind, and it caused her a lot of anxiety and worry. I tried to divert Mom's attention by changing the subject.

"Mom, remember I told you about my friend Karen from Los Angeles? Well, she's in San Diego right now with her husband, father, and their two children. They would like to meet us for dinner tonight at our hotel. Are you up for it?"

Mom said, "Sure, I remember you telling me before we left Vernon that we might have dinner with them while we were here. I'll try and come for a while, but I don't know how long I'll last."

"You certainly don't have to feel bad about not staying very long. If you get tired, we'll come back to the room."

Karen and I had been friends for close to twenty years. When I first met her, she had moved to Vernon from New York City for a year; then she moved to Los Angeles, where she met her husband. We had spoken on the phone many times since, but we hadn't seen each other face to face for more than five years. I was looking forward to catching up on what had been happening in her busy life.

As our meeting time approached, Mom and I went to the lobby to meet Karen and her family. I introduced Mom to everyone, and after the greetings died down, we walked through the lobby to the restaurant.

Mom enjoyed their company and especially liked Karen's father. The two of them had a lot in common. He had served in the Second World War as a pilot in the American Air Force, and since Mom had been in the British Army, they enjoyed a friendly debate on which was the better. Mom was quite charmed by him, and watching them together, I wished that she had not been so ill. I think if they had met under different circumstances, they would have enjoyed each other's company even more.

Mom began to fade around eight o'clock. I could see that it was time to say goodbye and get her to bed. I was sad to say goodbye to Karen and her family as I knew that it could be years before we saw each other again. So after lots of hugs, well wishes, and goodbyes we walked back to our room. Mom was exhausted. I could see that it had taken every ounce of determination to last throughout the visit. Seeing Mom so tired, I was thankful, that we were flying back to Canada in the morning.

Even though this trip had been initiated by a terrible illness, Mom said she enjoyed herself and felt that it had been somewhat of a holiday.

কৈত্ত

We boarded our plane early the next morning for what would be a very long day; we would not arrive back in Vernon until eight o'clock that night.

Buckling our seat belts, Mom said, "I'm sure looking forward to getting home. I can't handle this much activity anymore, no matter how enjoyable it is."

We settled back in our seats, and once we were in the air, we had a good laugh.

Mom was looking into her compact mirror, and as she was sliding her hand through her hair to tidy it up, she said, "Holy cow, I look like I've been dragged through a hedge backwards."

For some reason, this struck me as being so funny. I clearly visualized Mom being dragged backward through a bush with her hair sticking straight out and standing on end. Well, I started to laugh, and then she started to laugh. We began laughing louder and louder until we were both crying, with tears streaming down our cheeks. I looked around sheepishly. I realized we were being very noisy and saw a few of the passengers looking at us, wondering what was so funny. We quickly settled down and the rest of the trip went by without incident.

I was very happy that we would soon be on Canadian soil again and relieved that we would make it back without any major medical bills. This was a huge weight off my shoulders.

কৈত্ত

Just before landing at the Vancouver airport, the pilot's voice came over the loudspeaker saying that we were thirty minutes late. I immediately became concerned. How were we going to make our connecting flight? I called the flight attendant over and told her that we had to make our next flight because it was the last one of the day. She said she would call ahead, but we had to really hurry because the plane was scheduled to leave in fifteen minutes.

I had previously reserved a wheelchair for Mom upon landing, and once she was seated, I wheeled her up the ramp and into the main terminal. Running as quickly as I could, I arrived in front of the elevator. I pushed the button and then noticed a sign that said it was out of service.

Exasperated, I said "Oh damn! It's not working Mom, and we don't have time to find another lift. The only way to the departure lounge is the flight of stairs in front of us. Do you think you can walk up the stairs to the next level? I will do my best to get another wheelchair once I get to the top."

"I can make it, but I can't go very fast."

There were a lot of stairs ahead of her. I felt sick. I looked around for someone to help us, but there wasn't an attendant in sight. How was she going to handle all those stairs?

"Okay Mom, I'll take the bags and you take it easy."

She was exhausted, and yet here she was walking up the stairs to the terminal. I ran up the stairs, and when I got to the top I noticed a wheelchair for a different airline than ours. I hurried over to the counter and asked the attendant if I could borrow the wheelchair. I pointed over to Mom, just as she was taking the last step up to the landing, and told him that she was very ill and that we were late for our flight.

The man said, "If you're not travelling with our airline, you can't use it."

I could not believe his insensitivity; it was more than obvious that Mom was exhausted. I was so angry that I could not reply. I just glared at him in disgust and walked away.

By this time, I was getting desperate. Mom was really struggling and could not go any further.

Suddenly, out of the blue, an attendant from our airline was at our side with a wheelchair.

He said, "I'm sorry I took so long, but I didn't know where you were."

I was so surprised. I wondered how he knew that we needed a wheelchair, seeing as they had already given us one when we landed. How on earth did he know we were in trouble?

I said, "It's a miracle that you arrived when you did. I didn't think we were going to make our flight in time."

He whisked Mom through the airport to our departure gate, only to find that the plane had been delayed by twenty-five minutes.

I said to Mom, "That's so irritating! Why did they tell us that the flight was on time when it was actually close to half an hour late? If we had known that, we could have looked for a different elevator, and you wouldn't have tired yourself out. It would have been a lot less stressful."

Mom said, "Well, we're here now. We made it in time, and that's what counts. Carole, I'd love to have a coffee. Would you mind getting me one?"

I walked over to the coffee shop, came back and gave Mom her coffee, and said, "I'm just going to phone my friend Leigh for a quick chat. I'll be over by the window."

I kept my eye on Mom as she sat in the waiting area. I hung up from my call just in time to see Mom spill her coffee down one leg of her white pants. There was a brown stain from the top of her pants right down to her ankle.

I thought, Oh no, what next? I went over to her and asked what had happened.

She clicked her tongue and said, "The cup fell out of my hand. I'm so stupid. Look what I've done."

I was more than a little exasperated. The stress was wearing on me, and I was beginning to lose my patience. I sighed noisily and curtly asked, "How did it slip out of your hand? I'll go get something to clean it up."

So there was Mom, half brown and half white, boarding the plane. We both were definitely ready to go home to our separate places and have a break from each other. I was determined to give all her light-colored pants to the thrift shop when we got back. The white pants would have to go! The sole responsibility of taking care of my mother throughout this trip was weighing heavily on me. I was just so glad that we would soon be home.

~ ~

We arrived in Vernon to be greeted by Corky and two very excited kids. We collected our baggage, and as we were walking to the van, Corky leaned toward me and whispered, "What happened to your mom's pants?"

I glared at him and said, "Don't even ask!"

He stood back and said, "Why not?"

I said, "I really don't feel like talking about this right now! Please just drop it for now, okay?"

He put his hands up and said, "Sorry I asked!"

I felt terrible. He was so happy to see us, and I'd not been back more than twenty minutes and I had already snapped at him. I apologized and told him that I would talk about it later.

We drove Mom to her house. She had a lot of difficulty walking up the steps to her front door. She seemed to have lost much of her strength in the preceding five days.

As we brought her luggage into the house, she asked us to come in for a minute so that she could give the kids and Corky their presents. They opened their gifts and expressed their gratitude, and told her how much they loved them.

We made sure Mom was comfortable before we left. We said good night, and I promised to call her the next morning.

Chapter 9

A couple of days after arriving home from San Diego, Mom had an appointment with Doctor Morgan. We drove to his office, and I went in with her to talk the doctor. Mom relayed what the doctor in Mexico had recommended.

She said, "I'm ready to have another operation. I need to find a surgeon who is willing to attempt this."

After hesitating, he said, "Anne, I understand how you want to have this operation. We would give it to you if you weighed more, but right now you have absolutely no reserve. You weigh ninety-five pounds. Generally, people who have an operation like this can easily lose ten or more pounds while recuperating. You can't afford to lose that weight. If you could gain ten more pounds, maybe then we could think about it."

We both trusted Dr. Morgan. He was a wise and compassionate man, and we knew that he would do whatever he could to help Mom.

Leaving the doctor's office, I could see that she was very disheartened, and, in fact, Dr. Morgan looked very disheartened as well. I knew he wanted to help her, but his hands were tied. There wasn't anything he could do for her.

On the drive home, Mom said, "Maybe I could go to Vancouver and find a surgeon who would operate, but how can I trust them."

"I know you're really stuck, Mom. There's not much you can do but keep using the medicine from the clinic. What about using the shark cartilage the way they recently recommended?"

"Well, I'm going to give it a try. I don't have anything to lose."

I dropped Mom off at her house, and told her I would phone her later.

Driving home, I began mulling over all the things that had happened in the past eight months. Mom was fighting hard to live, never faltering in her determination to get well again. But I could see that we were now at a crossroads, not knowing which way to go. Were we losing the battle, or was there something else Mom could try?

Over the next two weeks, Mom administered the shark cartilage diligently, but I could tell that she was running out of steam and her enthusiasm was waning. She also came to the stark realization that she wasn't going to get the operation that she needed. It was obvious that her determination to cure this cancer was at an all-time low, and for that matter, so was mine.

I, too, was coming to the conclusion that Mom was losing the battle. I had to accept the fact that if she couldn't take the medicine from the clinic, she was not going to win. I had to accept that the fight was almost over, and I knew I had to change my attitude about what the outcome was going to be.

Mom had been re-evaluating her entire life since she had been diagnosed with cancer, and through this evaluation she had discovered a new attitude toward living. Now she would have to re-examine that attitude again. She would now have to learn how to die, and I knew that I would have to learn how to let her go. The thought that I was not going to have her with me for much longer was beginning to seep in; I felt overwhelmed by the deep sadness that enfolded me.

৯৹৹৻

It was September 6: the day before the kids started school for another year. We were sitting at the kitchen table having dinner when the kids began asking me a lot of questions about their Grandma. Tess was beginning to show the wear and tear of her Grandma being sick.

She asked, "Do you think Grandma's going to get better?"

I didn't want to lie to her. I said, "Tess, this is so difficult. I think we should be prepared for the fact that Grandma may not beat this cancer. She's worn out. She has fought long and hard, but this illness is getting to be too much for her."

Looking at me intently, her bottom lip began to tremble. As her eyes filled with tears, she got out of her chair and ran upstairs to her

79

bedroom, threw herself on the bed, and sobbed into her pillow. I quickly went up after her and sat beside her, rubbing her back.

She said, "If only Grandma had listened to us and quit smoking, she wouldn't be sick! Why did she have to smoke?"

She broke into tears again, and through muffled sobs she cried, "I don't want her to die!"

Trying to soothe her, I turned her over and held her while her little body shook from sobbing.

Doing my best to console her, I said, "Grandma is still alive, Tess. You still have her. She's not strong like she used to be, but who knows how long she has? She might be here longer than we think; we just have to be positive."

Tess said, "I know, but finally, Grandma moved back to Vernon and now she's sick. I was going to stay at her house overnight lots, without Nigel, and now I can't."

"I know, Tess. It's hard for all of us. I love Grandma so much too, and I feel angry like you. I feel as if we're being cheated out of having time with her."

I continued, "Do you remember that book we read? It talked about where people go after death? It said that a person doesn't really die; they just leave their bodies. If you want to be near them, you only have to think about them and they will be with you, even though you can't see them." I went on, "Well, I'd like to think that was true, so even though she's going to die sometime, all you have to do is think about her and she'll be with you."

Tess said, "I know, but I won't be able to hug her and sit on her knee any more or hold her hand."

My heart was breaking. I knew what she meant. Even though the idea that you didn't die sounded good, the bottom line was that you could not see or be with your loved ones anymore. That was a very difficult and different concept to cope with.

Tess wiped her tears away, sat up, and out of the blue said, "Can I phone Molly and see if she can come over?"

Surprised, I said, "Oh, sure, that's a good idea."

Children are remarkable. They have this wonderful knack of

being able to change moods instantaneously. One minute they are sobbing; the next minute they want to play. I was amazed at how much resilience Tess had amidst this painful situation. I watched Tess run down the stairs to call her friend and found myself wishing that I could be as easily appeased and distracted from the heavy things I had to bear.

Chapter 10

Mom continued to have difficulty with her diet. She was administering the shark cartilage as prescribed by the clinic, but she was still getting sick on a regular basis. She couldn't keep any food down. She began blaming the herbal medicine, saying that it didn't agree with her. But I knew that it was more than that. It was the blockage getting worse and the food was unable to get through her small intestine because of the tumor. The food had nowhere to go except back up.

Mom was more desperate than ever, and her extreme frustration was showing. I would make suggestions, and she would snap at me and say, "Carole, I've tried that. Don't keep on at me!"

Under normal circumstances, she would never have responded that way. I knew she was sick and tired of the whole ordeal and felt downright miserable. The realization that she was losing the battle was setting in. She hadn't said that she was going to give up, but I could see that she was not trying as hard. She was using the shark cartilage, but less consistently.

One day I phoned her at the same time she was mixing the shark cartilage into a paste. She was very irritated.

This is so frustrating! I'm getting sick and tired of doing this."

"I know Mom, but if it works, then it's going to be worth it."

"I just don't know if I can do this anymore."

I knew, then, that Mom was tired of the battle. She was resigning herself to the illness and was at a crossroads as to whether she wanted to fight anymore. I don't believe this was a conscious decision at the time, but I could hear in her voice that she was beginning to change her thoughts about living and dying.

She had tried so hard; I had tried so hard. My mom's battle had become mine, and, for that matter, a battle for the whole family. Each little bit of hope that had been given over the past eight months had made me as excited as Mom, and every little bit of bad news had made me just as depressed as she was. We were on a roller-coaster ride, up and down, and it seemed these days, that there were more downs than ups.

ॐॐ

One day while visiting Mom at her home, I asked her if she had cried very much since she found out she had cancer.

She said, "You know Carole, I've hardly cried at all. It's as if I have no tears. I guess I feel that there's no point in feeling sorry for myself. There's nothing that benefits me through negative feelings."

I said, "Maybe so, but crying can be a really good release for pent-up emotions. I always feel better after I cry. It's a good release."

She responded, "Well I think if I started to cry, really cry, I wouldn't be able to stop."

"I know, Mom. I'm sure you have years of pain held deep inside. I read somewhere cancer is partly emotional: holding our emotions inside. I don't know how true that statement is, but it's something to think about."

Mom said, "Yes, that would be me. I have spent my life holding my feelings inside and not saying anything, even though I felt hurt or sad, or even when I was mad. I didn't want to create conflict, so I would just try and forget whatever it was that upset me."

I said, "I can see that about you. When I was young, I remember you as such an easy going person; you rarely lost your temper. I can see that you've spent a lifetime thinking about other people to the point that you stayed in a bad marriage because of Vern and me. You let Dad call all the shots."

Mom added, "Well, in those days men were the boss and did call the shots. Most women I knew didn't fight back. But more than that, I just couldn't bear any fighting. I hate confrontation, and it just seemed easier to give in than to argue."

"If that's the case, I wonder why you chose such a strong-willed husband."

"It's strange isn't it? Looking back, I wanted to leave your Dad when Vern was two years old; I knew then that I had made a mistake, but I had nowhere to go. I didn't have family in Canada; they were all living in England. And at that time, women didn't work much, if at all, and single mothers were unheard of unless you were a widow. I would have been considered a black sheep, so I stayed and made the best of it. I was a good actress in those days; even my friends didn't know I was unhappy. I put on a pretty good face back then."

Mom went on, "Since I've been ill, I can see now how much I believed that I was a weak person. There's an old saying that would often ring in my ear: 'You make your bed; you lie in it'. That's how I was raised. I had you and Vern to think about, so I stayed with your Dad until you were in your mid-twenties, and then that was it. I finally found enough courage to ask him to leave."

I said, "I can hardly believe that you thought you were weak. You started working outside of the home when I was seven years old. Dad worked at the paper and was only home on weekends for close to twenty years. You basically raised Vern and me on your own. When I was seventeen, you supported the family on your wages when Dad retired with a small pension."

I continued, "That, Mom, is not a weak person. And look at you now! You have been an incredible inspiration to everyone. "You are handling this illness with so much courage and grace. You have been so strong, so determined, and so positive. The pain you have been through would have put me under ten times over, and on top of it all, you hardly ever complain. But saying all that, maybe that's part of the pattern you have developed because of your marriage. You're just sucking it up, not showing your true feelings about being ill."

"Yes I do hide a lot of my feelings, I guess it has become a big part of who I am, and I doubt that part of my personality will ever change. But I do see now that I'm not as weak as I thought, even though, unfortunately, it's taken me seventy years and cancer to figure that out. It's too bad I had to find out this way."

"Well, other people see your strength and courage. The home care nurses have told me what a special person you are. They said that many of the patients they see are demanding and miserable, but not you; you always have a smile and something positive to say."

Mom said, "Well, what's the point in being miserable? I admit that I don't show how I'm really feeling, but I don't think it is right to take out my misery on other people. But, saying that, the challenges have been so overwhelming at times. I sometimes feel like I am in a horrible nightmare."

I said, "Well, I've believed for many years that the journey of life is overcoming the challenges that come before us, and through those challenges we learn about what we're really made of, who we really are. Every one of us is going to have to face our mortality; what's happening to you is going to happen to everyone. Maybe not cancer, but we are all going to die from something."

Mom replied, "Yes, death was the last thing I thought about when I was healthy. Dealing with the face of death has really made me stop and look at my life. I have learned a lot about myself over this last year. I have been thinking about my childhood and how I was raised. I had a strong, domineering father who was very strict, and because of that, I always did what I was told. I never talked back or argued with him. When I think about it, that's probably why I attracted your father. I was used to that kind of male figure. I think your dad was attracted to me because he could see how passive I was. He would boss me around and I wouldn't fight back. She paused and then went on, "But the one thing I really liked about your Dad was that he treated you differently than how my father treated me. You were the apple of your Dad's eye. I was always amazed at how he tolerated you talking back to him. You always had the courage to stand up to him."

I said, "Yeah, he did allow me to have my own opinion; but at the same time, he tried to boss me around, too. I guess I knew his bark was much worse than his bite, and I may have taken advantage of that. Looking back, I can see that he should've disciplined me more for talking back to him, especially in my teens."

"I'll agree to that," Mom added jokingly. "Your Dad never could stay mad at you; he always gave in to you."

"Yeah, I think the one time that really stands out for me, was when I was sixteen. I smashed the tail light on his beloved, precious Lincoln, and I put all the pieces on the floor of the garage, below the broken light. I was trying to set up a crime scene that someone must have come into the garage and broke it. Of course he knew I had done it. He sat me down in the living room and gave me a long lecture. I was certain I would be in the doghouse for at least a month and wouldn't be allowed to drive his car for a very long time. To my surprise, once he was finished his lecture, he threw me the keys and twenty bucks and told me I could have the car. He was so lenient with me."

Mom said, "I remember that story; your dad really did have a good heart. But there was another side to him that I found difficult. He loved debating politics and religion and was always trying to drag me into his discussions. That's when I would disappear into the bedroom and put my head in a book."

"Yes, I do remember you hiding out in the bedroom, lying on the bed and reading."

She said, "You remember that? Hmmm, when I think about it, I guess I have spent most of my life behind books. If I could do it differently, I would change that behavior. Instead of hiding away, I would be more courageous and not be afraid to make changes in my life. I know I've said this plenty of times over the last year, but I should have retired five years ago. I was so afraid that I didn't have enough money. This is one of the biggest regrets I have."

"I know, Mom. That has been a really big one for you. We all have many 'should haves,' but we can't dwell on the past. There's that old saying, 'Hindsight is 20/20'." Pausing, I said, "But it does make me wonder why we can't see clearly at the time and why we stay in bad situations even when we are unhappy. We are so afraid to step into the unknown: it seems we want security over happiness.

"Well, that would be me in a nutshell, always wanting security and safety." With a touch of sarcasm she added, "And where did that get me in the end?"

"You're not alone. Mom, I think that is a very common sentiment."

She stifled a yawn and said with resignation, "Oh well, you can't cry over spilt milk."

I could see that Mom was getting sleepy.

She said, "I'm going to have a nap. I'm tired."

"Alright, I have to go anyway, Mom. I'll call you later."

Driving home, I thought about how much I enjoyed this talk with Mom. It was a complete surprise to me that she saw herself as weak. I had always seen her as a very strong, stable person who had been, and still was, an excellent role model. She'd always been there for me my entire life; she was my rock.

I pondered how often we perceive ourselves incorrectly, and, really, how blind we can be about our own strengths and weaknesses.

Chapter 11

September was Mom's favorite month. The weather in Vernon is usually perfect with warm, sunny days, and this fall was no exception. The month flew by in a whirl of activity. The kids were back in school and busy with their extracurricular activities. I was busy as their chauffeur.

At this time, Mom's best friend, Cathy, wanted to help out and offered to stay with Mom three days a week. They went shopping, out for lunch, and to the casino to play bingo. Mom hadn't been a bingo player before her illness, but now she enjoyed the outing. Just getting out of the house was a treat for her.

At the end of September, after one of her visits with Mom, Cathy phoned me, very concerned.

She said, "Anne seems to be getting weaker by the day, Carole. She's finding it difficult to walk up the stairs to her front door. I've been making sure she gets her high-calorie drinks a couple of times a day, but it doesn't seem to give her that much-needed strength or keep her energy level up. I think she is losing weight, rather than gaining it."

"I know, Cathy. I am at a loss as to what I can do to help her get her strength back. I think we've tried just about everything."

Cathy said, "Well, we'll just keep working at it, that's all we can do."

Mom was increasingly more agitated and irritable. It was becoming evident that Mom's focus of attention was changing. She was starting to worry about unfinished projects that needed to be done around her house. I would remind her that things that were bothering her around the house were not important and to just enjoy the lovely fall days. However, it didn't matter what I said, she was set on having these chores completed without delay.

I was confused by her changing behavior, so I phoned Vern to discuss this new situation with him.

"You know Vern, it's the strangest thing. I'm sure Mom knows that she only has a short time to live, yet she's majorly anxious about completing insignificant projects around her house."

"That doesn't make sense to me. If I were dying, that would be the last thing I'd care about. Maybe she's having a hard time thinking clearly these days."

"No, I don't think that's it. She seems the same in every other way except for the anxiety she's feeling about fixing her house."

Vern said, "I talked to Mom yesterday, and told her I was coming to visit, sometime in the next two weeks. I'll call her after I hang up with you and let her know that I will help her with anything that she needs done around her place. If these things are important to her, then we had better help her out."

"That would be a load off my shoulders if you did these projects. I don't have the time or the energy and neither does Corky. To be honest, I'm so stressed out and tired from this roller-coaster ride. To top it all off, I found out today that the college neglected to tell me I am missing one course, so I don't have my Certification for teaching. Talk about bad timing. Just the thought of having to do papers and study again really exhausts me. I almost feel like putting it off until next year."

"Don't do that. I'll help you as much as I can. You've had the bulk of this on your shoulders, and you shouldn't have to give up any more than you already have."

I conceded, "Oh, I'm just whining and feeling sorry for myself right now. I'll take the course. I know I'd be mad at myself if I didn't persevere and finish it this year. It just makes me tired thinking about all the extra work."

"Well, I'll be there soon to relieve you for awhile. Those projects will give me something to do when I'm visiting. Now, off the subject, I'll bring you guys some fresh oysters and a big salmon and we can have a seafood feast."

"Great, that would be a nice treat. You bring them; I'll cook them!"

৵৽

The next afternoon, I drove to Mom's house for a visit. I found her in the yard, dozing on her outdoor lounger. I noticed she was wearing a pair of diamond earrings that sparkled brightly in the sun. For some reason, this sight brought back a memory of when I was nine years old, and our family was in the car driving to a friend's house.

It had been a sunny, warm day and I was sitting in the back seat with Vern. Mom had worn a white summer dress accented with a blue and green crystal necklace and a pair of matching earrings. As we were driving, the sun's rays caught the stones and cast large, brilliant light balls over the entire inside roof of the car. Every time she moved, they would glimmer and sparkle and streak across the seats and doors. It was such a beautiful sight to behold. This memory reminded me of the many times in my life that I had admired how beautiful she was. She was always perfectly dressed, not a hair out of place. Even today, she still looked elegant—coiffed and dressed impeccably.

Mom heard me as I walked toward her; she opened her eyes and smiled.

I sat down beside her and said, "Hi Mom, how are you today?"

"Not bad. I'm getting a few cramps, and my bag seems to be filling up slower than usual. I feel so tired, and I seem to be falling asleep all the time. She paused, "You know, I've been lying here thinking how wrong the doctors were. After my last operation they told me I had three months to live, but look, I'm still alive."

I was taken aback. All I could do was fake a positive response, "Yep Mom, they sure were wrong."

I couldn't say much more than that. I didn't want to upset her by reminding her that the surgeon had said she had three to six months to live, and it had only been four months ago that he gave that diagnosis.

My God, I thought, she doesn't realize how sick she really is. She's talking like she's still going to make it.

I really didn't know what to say. She still believed she wasn't going to die any time soon. She was in denial. I didn't want to pop her bubble, and I certainly didn't want to take her hope away; after all, that was all she had left.

At that moment, Dr. Morgan drove into the driveway. He had arrived for his weekly visit to check on Mom. He walked over to us, sat down on one of the outdoor chairs, and asked, "How are you feeling, Anne?"

She said, "I'm still getting a lot of cramps; the painkillers don't seem to be helping as much anymore. And I have to be very careful as to what I eat. I'm basically on a liquid diet now, but even then, I still get sick every couple of days."

Dr. Morgan said, "If a liquid diet works the best for you, then you should continue with it."

Mom interjected, "But why am I getting sick so much when all I'm ingesting is liquid?"

He gently said, "The tumor may be getting larger, and this is stopping the food from going through your intestines. The only place it can go is back up into the stomach, and then you're getting sick."

He pulled out a prescription pad and said, "I'm going to give you morphine. Take a teaspoonful when you're in pain. It can make you quite drowsy, so it's best to take it when you aren't going out."

"What, I thought. She's going to be here alone, drugged on morphine?

I interrupted, "The home care nurse comes twice daily for a short visit, but what about the rest of the time when she's here by herself? If Mom's taking morphine on a regular basis, she will need a lot more supervision. I think she should stay at our house."

Mom adamantly said, "Carole, I don't want to leave my house. I'm fine here alone; I can take care of myself. I enjoy being by myself, and I like my privacy. I can do what I want, when I want. I can watch television and not be bothered, or for that matter, bother anyone."

I argued, "I know, Mom, and I do understand how important it is for you to be independent; but at the same time, I will worry about you taking morphine while you are alone. I will make sure you have as much privacy as you want at our house and make sure that the kids don't bother you."

She was adamant. "No, I want to stay here. I'll be fine."

Dr. Morgan continued, "Carole, if Anne is happy here, then I can't see any reason for her to come and stay with you."

"What about the morphine? She could accidently take too much and end up hurting herself."

He said, "If Anne uses it correctly, it shouldn't be a problem."

I felt that what Dr. Morgan was saying was wrong. I was perturbed that he was not thinking of her safety.

He stood up, and said he had to leave but would come by the house to see Mom the following week. I walked him to his car, and as he opened the car door, he said, "I don't think your mother has too much time left. But she is a strong woman with a very strong will to live. She could last another month, but, again, it's hard to say."

I asked, "Why did you disagree with me about Mom staying with us now that she's taking morphine?"

He said kindly, "I agreed with your mom because she wants her independence. She is seventy years old and has taken care of herself for most of her life. I just don't want to see her lose her positive spirit. She has a little time left, so why not let her do what she wants?"

I reluctantly admitted, "I guess you're right, but I think it could be dangerous for Mom to be alone while taking morphine. I will worry that she has taken too much. And on top of that, it's a lot of work driving back and forth to her home all the time. It would be so much easier to have her at my house." I took a deep breath and went on, "I know that is selfish on my part, but at the same time, I am taking care of a young family and a terminally ill parent. I really am exhausted, and now I feel I will worry even more."

Dr. Morgan put his hand on my shoulder and said, "Carole, this is probably one of the toughest times in your life. I do understand how hard this is for you. But let your mom come to that place on her own—where she doesn't feel safe alone anymore and wants to finally leave her home for the last time. I know that day will come in the near future. Just give her some time."

I thanked Dr. Morgan for his wise words and said goodbye.

I returned to where Mom was sitting. She looked up from her

magazine and said, "Carole, don't worry so much, I'll be fine. I love my home, and I feel happier here than anywhere else right now."

"I know, Mom. I concede and I do understand. I just want you to know that if it gets to be too much for you, you are welcome at a moment's notice to come and stay at our house."

"I know and I appreciate that honey, thank you."

Over the last few weeks, Mom had mentioned several times that she didn't want to drive her car anymore because it made her nervous. This was such a relief to us all. We were glad she had come to that conclusion herself, instead of the family having to tell her. If there was ever a doubt about this decision, the morphine prescription had definitely put an end to Mom getting behind the wheel anytime soon.

ॐॐ

By this time, it was the first week of October. Mom finally had x-rays of her abdomen taken. She needed to have proof that there really was a tumor.

She said, "Carole, I need your help if you don't mind. I have to pick up my x-rays tomorrow and bring them to Dr. Morgan so he can go over the results with me. I want to see for myself what's happening with my stomach."

"That's a really good idea."

Suddenly Mom's demeanor changed. She appeared deflated and said, "I can't seem to keep anything I eat or drink in my stomach. I'm getting sick all the time now." With anguish she said, "I'm so bloody tired of being sick!"

She put her face in her hands and burst into tears. I quickly went over to her and put my arm around her shoulder. She sobbed and sobbed, and then taking a few deep breaths she composed herself enough to say, "I can't take this anymore. When is this going to end? I just don't know why this is happening to me. This is so dehumanizing!"

"Damn it, Mom, I don't know why, either. I truly wish we could

93

wake up tomorrow morning and find that this was all just a bad dream. I hate to see you suffer. You don't deserve this at all."

Mom wiped her tears and said, "I must have done something really awful, to be dying like this. I had always wanted to die quietly in my sleep. Never in my wildest imagination did I think this would happen to me."

"Mom, you didn't do anything bad. Let's face it; the odds were stacked against you from the beginning with your family history. I guess I could be a candidate for bowel cancer at some point in my life, too. I've tried not to think about that, but the thought does seep in every once in a while. I never worried much about cancer before you were diagnosed. I thought that it was other people who got cancer. This has been a rude awakening on so many levels for all of us."

Mom said, "I don't understand why people have to suffer like this. It makes me wonder about God, or even if there is a God."

"Since you've been sick, I have wondered the same thing. But there has to be a reason that we go through painful, challenging times. I can't help but think that there must be a plan for each of us. Look at how much you and I have grown this last year, especially you Mom. Your perception about yourself and your life has changed dramatically; you have discovered so much strength and determination.

Mom said, "That's true, I guess. I have found myself thinking a lot about where I fit into this universe and wonder if there is something more out there for me. I find myself feeling that this body isn't really me; sometimes I feel like I am just borrowing it. I can see that I am so much more than this body, but at the same time, I don't have a clue what any of that means."

She went on, "Cancer has really forced me to focus on my mortality and whether there is life after this life. I've been learning so much about myself and who I am. At the same time, it saddens me because I learned this too late, and now I won't be able to use any of the new-found wisdom in my future because the truth is, I have no future."

"I don't think you lose any of the wisdom that has been acquired in a lifetime. I believe we take everything we've learned with us. Nothing is lost; it's called evolution."

"I hope you are right. You know, I sold hundreds of books on the subject of life after death, and yet I rarely read any of them."

"Well, like I said, it's never too late. You might find that they help you."

"I'll think about it. I can't seem to read any of the books I have right now. I don't know why, but I seem to have lost the ability to concentrate ever since my first operation."

We quietly sat together for a moment, both lost in our own thoughts, pondering what had been said. I found myself thinking about how different we were from each other. I had shared information with Mom over the years about the many metaphysical and spiritual books I had read, but she was never interested. She would say that she believed in God, but it wasn't necessary to study or read books to be spiritual. I, on the other hand, had spent a large part of my life searching for answers to my existence.

I remembered back to when I was twenty years old. I had travelled overland from Greece to Afghanistan to learn about the Sufis, then on to India where I spent time with a guru who taught Vipassana meditation. I had stayed at his ashram for weeks, meditating for many hours a day and committing to absolute silence. I spent a year travelling through India and Sri Lanka and then settled in Katmandu for three months, living alone in a tiny shack in the Himalayas.

Looking back, I could see how many years I'd been searching for answers as to who I was and why I was here. It seemed it had been most of my life. I realized then that I still didn't have a clue as to what life was all about.

Returning from my thoughts, I asked, "Mom, are you afraid to die? Does it scare you?"

"I try not to think about it," she answered. "I find myself wondering if there really is anything after you die. Maybe there is nothing. Maybe I'll be nothing after I die. I'll just ... poof ... disappear without a trace."

I disagreed, "Mom, no way. But you know how I think. I believe that your physical body dies but you don't. You're going to leave a very tired and ill body, and when you're finally liberated from your body, you're going to be so happy. You're going to be as free as a bird!"

She chuckled and shook her head, "Carole, honestly, the way you think sometimes."

"You wait and see. You'll be up there, looking down on me and saying, 'You know, that daughter of mine wasn't as crazy as I thought. She was right; it's great to be out of the body. I don't mind this at all!'"

We both laughed, and Mom said, "Well, I guess we'll just have to wait and see, won't we?"

She changed the subject and said, "My appointment with Dr. Morgan is tomorrow at one o'clock. Could you take me?"

"Sure. I'll come by and get you around twelve-thirty." Looking at my watch, I said, "It's getting late. I had better get home to Corky and the kids."

೭ం◌ఄ

That evening, shortly after dinner, Tess and I had an argument. I was irritated that her room was such a mess, and I angrily told her to clean it up. She ran upstairs to her room, yelling at me, "You're so mean!" and slammed the door.

I chased after her and said, "Listen young lady, don't you yell at me, and don't you slam this door. I won't have it."

She lay crying on her bed. She sobbed, "I wish Grandma was dead. I hate this. You're not even my mom anymore. You're always grouchy and you're never here. You're always at Grandma's house."

I was completely stunned. I knew that Tess adored her Grandma and that this outburst was caused by all the pain she was feeling over her Grandma being ill. I sat down on her bed and rubbing her back, I said, "Tess I'm so sorry; I know I haven't been myself. But I never realized I was upsetting you so much."

"Well, you are. You never talk to me anymore. You're always too tired."

"I guess I am tired a lot. Grandma's illness has been hard on me, and there isn't anyone else to take care of her, so I have to do it all myself. The thought of her being alone and not seeing her every day would be difficult for me."

Tess said, "I know Mom. I didn't mean that I wish Grandma would die. I just wish that she would get better and that she wasn't sick."

She started to sob again. I held her tight.

"I know honey. It's so hard to think about her not being here anymore. I don't know what we're going to do without her. I'm really sorry for the way I have been. I've been under so much stress lately. I'm really glad you told me how you are feeling, and I will try not to be so grouchy."

Wiping her tears, Tess asked, "How long is Grandma going to live?"

I found it difficult to give a specific answer. It couldn't be more than a month, but I skirted around the subject and said, "I'm not sure, but we should try and spend as much time as we can with her."

I changed the subject and said, "It's late Tess, and you had better go to sleep. Don't worry about your room tonight; we'll clean it up together tomorrow. I love you. See you in the morning."

Chapter 12

The next morning, I drove Mom to her very important doctor's appointment. We picked up her x-rays at the radiology clinic and then drove to the doctor. We arrived just in time to go into his office.

Once Mom was on the examination table, Dr. Morgan palpated Mom's abdomen and then measured the size of the tumor. Unfortunately, it had grown. When he'd finished his assessment, Mom got down from the table and sat in the chair beside his desk. Dr. Morgan put the x-rays up to a light box and pointed to a dark area on the screen.

He began his explanation by saying, "This gray and black area is where the tumor sits. It has grown under your ribs and half-way over your abdomen. Your small intestine is being blocked by the tumor, and that's why your food won't stay down."

Mom sat quietly for a moment and then asked, "Could I have an operation to cut the tumor out?"

With a touch of sadness, he said, "Anne, you wouldn't survive an operation. You are far too weak." He hesitated and then went on, "I think you should just try and enjoy the time you have left."

Mom took a deep breath and asked, "Tell me honestly. How much time do I have left?"

"Anne, it is so hard to predict. You could have one month; maybe two."

Mom slowly stood up from the chair. I could see by the expression on her face that reality had finally sunk in. There really was a tumor; she could see it on the x-ray as plain as day. There was no hope left. Mom slowly turned toward the door, thanked the Doctor and walked out of the office and into the waiting room.

I stayed behind for a few moments to ask, "Do you really feel she will live for another two months?"

"I don't want to take away your mother's hope," he replied, "That's all she has. When a person has a very strong will to live, it is hard to say what will happen. After examining your mother today and seeing how thin she is, I would say she has maybe one month at the most. But as you can see, your mother is not ready to die yet. Acceptance of one's death is an ongoing process, and it takes time. Let her come to this realization on her own."

"Well, Dr. Morgan, she's a real fighter, and you're right about not wanting to take her hope away. I'll try and support this process as much as I can. Thanks for giving Mom another x-ray. I think it makes it more comprehensible and real for her."

We left the office, and on our way home, Mom threw me for a loop when she said, "So, Dr. Morgan said that I could go along like this for months. I'll just keep drinking those high-calorie drinks. Who knows what could happen."

I was stunned. I couldn't believe what I was hearing. Hadn't she listened to anything the doctor had just told her? She was still denying the fact that she was not going to live much longer.

The stress of her illness was starting to take its toll on me, and who was I kidding anyway. I knew that Mom was not going to live much longer, but why couldn't she see that? Why wasn't she willing to give up this fight and enjoy the little time she had left? I really wished that she would accept the fact that it would soon be over. I just couldn't believe that she was still in so much denial.

As my disbelief subsided, I began to feel guilty that I had these kinds of thoughts. I didn't want her to die. I just wanted our lives to go back to normal. I just wanted her back the way she was.

I drove Mom to her house, gave her a hug, and said, "See you tomorrow. Call me if you need anything. Hang in there Mom."

With a determined voice she said, "You bet I will."

As I drove out of her driveway, I couldn't help but feel deep admiration for her. She never burdened anyone with her pain. She was always so composed and optimistic. But underneath that positive front, I wondered what she really felt when she closed the door to the outside world and she was all alone. Did she break down and cry? Was she devastated? Was she afraid? I was pretty sure that I would never find that out; she would never show me that she was crushed.

She was still the mother and I was the daughter, and she was not going to relinquish that role unless it was absolutely necessary.

കൈ

That night after dinner, there was only one thing I wanted to do and that was to curl up on the couch with a cozy blanket and watch a movie. Just as I was in the process of ordering a comedy, the phone rang; it was Mom in distress.

"You have to come and get me; I'm in terrible pain! I have to go to the hospital right away."

I jumped up off the couch and said, "Mom, I'll be right there!"

I raced out the door and drove to her house in record time. I quickly ran into the living room and found her doubled over in immense pain. With great difficulty, I helped her into the van and thought, Oh God, I hope her bowel didn't rupture again!

Mom was admitted into the hospital and on to a ward right away. She was writhing in so much pain that the nurse had to administer a high dose of pain medication. I couldn't take seeing her in this kind of agony, and it took every bit of self control to stop from bursting into tears.

Once Mom was calm, I looked around the room and saw an acquaintance of mine, sitting with her Mom in an adjacent bed. I wasn't in the mood to talk, and I hoped that she didn't see me. However, while I was hanging Mom's clothes in the closet, she walked over to me and cheerfully said, "Hi Carole. It's so nice to see you. This is so funny; both of our Moms are here in the same room together."

Her cheerfulness was too much for me. It was obvious that her Mom wasn't dying and mine was. A huge lump began forming in my throat and my eyes began filling with tears. I looked down and mumbled, "Please excuse me, but I can't talk right now."

I turned and stumbled into the bathroom, closed the door, and sobbed. I slid down the wall and sat on the floor beside the toilet for the longest time with streams of tears falling down my cheeks. I really couldn't handle any of this anymore. I was falling apart.

It took me a good ten minutes before I realized that I had to get out of the bathroom. I took a few deep breaths, stood up and looked at myself in the mirror, and thought, "Wow, I really look a mess." I blew my nose, washed my face, straightened myself as best I could, and then walked out into the hospital room. Luckily, my friend had left.

I went over to Mom and held her hand. The nurse was giving Mom more pain medication. She said, "Your mom is doing better. We've given her another dose of pain medication."

Suddenly, with urgency Mom said, "Quick, give me the pan! I'm going to be sick!"

Mom began throwing up. I carried pan after pan of this watery liquid to the toilet. As I walked back and forth, to and from the bathroom, tears began streaming down my face, and at that point I really didn't care who saw me.

The nurse took me aside and asked, "Are you all right?"

"I'm okay. It's just that I can't stop crying. I've had to watch my mom suffer for so long. How much more can she take? I'm sorry I'm such a mess, but I guess the strain of it all has hit me hard today."

She squeezed my arm and said, "Don't be hard on yourself; this is tough stuff you're dealing with."

After about an hour, as the pain and throwing up subsided, Mom could finally rest. I sat by her bed and held her hand, and said, "It's so hard to see you struggle with so much pain and nausea. I find it so frustrating that I can't do anything to stop your suffering."

"Oh Carole, I'm so sorry for putting you through this. I never wanted to be a burden to you, and now look—I've caused you so much sorrow and hardship," she said.

"Mom, I'm not going through anything compared to you. You hurt so much. I hate God. How could he let people suffer like this?"

Mom squeezed my hand and smiled, "I thought you said that everything happens for a reason."

"Well, right now, I've just changed my mind. As far as I'm concerned, this is nuts; no one should have to go through this kind of suffering."

"Yes," she said sleepily, "I had no idea what being sick really meant. I've always been so healthy."

"You need to rest Mom. I'll come by tomorrow."

Mom barely whispered a "good night." She was heavily sedated and was falling asleep. So with her out of pain and at ease, I left the hospital around ten o'clock, drove home, and fell into bed. I was beat.

Chapter 13

I returned to the hospital early the next morning to find Mom getting sick.

Alarmed, I asked, "Have you been doing this all night?"

"No" she answered. "It started again about ten minutes ago. I think I'm okay now. I must have eaten too much breakfast."

"Thank goodness! Has the pain stopped?"

"The pain has subsided a lot, and I feel much better."

"Well that's a relief. Have you had a lot of pain medication today?"

"No," she said. "They've changed my medication and put an analgesic patch on my shoulder that allows small amounts of pain medication into my system, and it seems to be working."

I said, "These patches sound very promising. I've never heard of them before."

"Doctor Morgan said that they've been around for awhile. The patch seems to be keeping the pain under control. I feel tired but not drugged like I did with the injections."

Mom changed the subject and said, "They took another x-ray this morning. I've had so many x-rays this year that if the cancer doesn't kill me, the x-rays will."

We both chuckled. I said, "I doubt that the x-rays have done that much harm, but I know what you mean; you've certainly had your share of them. Have you seen Doctor Morgan this morning?"

"Yes, he came in earlier. He's such a wonderful doctor with such good bedside manners. If only I were forty years younger!"

I said, "Yes, he is quite cute!" We both laughed.

Mom continued, "He said that the x-ray revealed that my small intestine ruptured again because of the blockage. It seems there is now a hole in my intestine that goes into my stomach, so now when I eat, the food goes down into my intestine and then comes back into my stomach, and then I throw up what I ate."

I was aghast. I couldn't believe what I was hearing; never had I heard of anything as bizarre as this. How could a person still be alive after so many traumas to the vital organs?

"Mom, how can you be so calm?"

"Well, believe it or not, I feel a lot better since the pressure has gone. The rupturing of my intestine must have stopped the pain I had last night. Dr. Morgan said that I am very lucky because if my bowel had ruptured into the abdominal cavity, I would have died from a massive infection."

I didn't know what to say. I still had her for a while longer, but in what state. The thought of all of this was beyond my comprehension. How much more could she endure?

At that moment, I found myself wondering what the hell life was all about. I looked around the hospital room. Many of the beds were filled with seniors who were terminally ill and didn't have family to take care of them. I felt very sad for these patients; this was the end of the road for them. They would die in a cold and lonely hospital by themselves, without any loved ones around them. So many people die like this. Why did they have to suffer so much, and what was to be gained by it all?

I looked out the door of Mom's room and saw a lady in her late eighties sitting in the hallway in a chair, furiously rocking back and forth yelling, "Help me, help me!" The nurses would ignore her as long as they could before telling her to be quiet. Supposedly she did this off and on throughout the day, every day.

Other seniors on the ward weren't ill but needed supervision and had been admitted to the hospital while waiting for a bed to open up at one of the senior citizen homes in town. The nurses told me that many of these patients rarely got visitors. They just sat and stared out the window, walked the halls, or watched television for most of the day. They looked depressed and sad, and it was clearly seen in their faces that they had given up on life.

My thoughts came back to Mom. She was not at all like them. She still had this fighting, positive spirit and she was not going to give up any time soon.

I turned to Mom and asked, "Did the doctor give you some kind of a prognosis?"

She leaned back on her pillow and said, "This is the way it is, there is no turning back." She took a deep breath and said, "I'm lucky to be alive at all, and fortunately I still have some time left."

I held her hand, trying to hide my deep sadness. She was deteriorating and wasting away to nothing; she weighed less than ninety pounds. It had become difficult for her to walk to the bathroom because she was so weak, and here she was, telling me how lucky she was.

How could she be so positive when the future looked so grim? I wondered if I would have had that type of optimism if I had been in the same situation. I doubted it very much.

I stayed at the hospital until it was time to pick the kids up from school. When I got home, I phoned Vern and told him how Mom's small intestine had ruptured again and that he should come to see her as soon as possible.

He said, "I can't believe she is still alive with a hole in her stomach. That is so bizarre, Carole. It's like some kind of nightmare! Who can live with this type of sickness?"

He went on, "I'll come to Vernon as soon as I can get some of my bookwork straightened out, hopefully by the beginning of next week. I think that's October 30. I'll come up for seven or eight days."

"I'm so glad you can come back again. But in the meantime, I'm getting a moving company to bring Mom's bed from her spare room back to our house. Hopefully, she will come to her senses and stay with us for the remainder of the time she has left. She is in no shape to stay alone, believe me."

Vern said, "That would be great if she could stay with you. She shouldn't be by herself at her house. When I come next week, I'll take her home and stay with her while I am there."

"That would be great! Thanks for coming on such short notice. You don't know how much I appreciate being able to have a break."

"Carole, believe me, I can't imagine what you must be feeling.

It's been such a long haul for you. It won't be long before I am there to relieve you. See you in a few days."

ॐ◆ॐ

I drove to Mom's house the next morning to meet the moving company and get Mom's bed. They loaded up the truck and followed me back to my house. Once everything was in place, I went to the hospital.

When I walked into Mom's room, I noticed she was very distant and not as friendly as usual. I cheerfully said, "Hi Mom, how are you?"

Barely glancing at me, she said, "Oh, not too bad."

Then, to my surprise, Mom looked up at me and said, "Listen Carole, you don't have to keep coming here all the time. There's no point in you sitting here hour after hour with nothing to do. I really have nothing to say anymore, and I would like to be left alone. I really don't feel like visitors or talking to anyone."

"You don't have to talk to me, Mom. I don't like you being alone, and I know how much you hate it here."

Mom adamantly said, "Carole, I don't want to visit right now."

Her words went through me like a knife. I felt hurt by her words and distant, cold demeanor.

I said, "Okay, that's fine."

I got up off the chair, said goodbye and left. As I walked out of the room, I could feel many different emotions churning around inside me: anger, sadness, fear, and rejection.

I went home and told Corky what Mom had said to me, and how she seemed very indifferent and cold.

He said, "She must be coming to the realization that she is dying, and this is probably causing her to withdraw. I expect she's going through every emotion imaginable. Let's face it; we have rarely seen her upset since she found out she had cancer. She's been through a hell of a lot, so I think you need to be patient with her. I'll come with you and talk to her tonight."

After dinner, Corky and I went to the hospital. I sat outside the

106

room while he went in to talk to Mom. Even though I knew she must be really upset, I didn't understand why she was pushing me away.

After ten minutes or so, Corky called me into the room. I walked in and stood tentatively by Mom's bed.

Mom smiled at me and put her hand on mine, and said, "Carole, I was just telling Corky that I didn't mean to upset you. I'm sick and tired of this whole thing. This is a miserable way to die, especially when I'm just not ready. I had so many plans, so much to live for, and now they're all gone. I'm trying to sort my feelings out. I have to face up to the fact that I'm not going to live much longer."

"I understand, Mom; I can't imagine how difficult this is for you."

"Please don't get your feelings hurt. Don't get me wrong; you've been so good to me, and I know you have my best interests at heart." She paused and said, "Now, it's important that you understand that I've decided to stay at your house for a few days, and then I want to go back to my place. Vern will be there with me, so you don't have to worry. I won't be alone."

"That sounds fine to me. I'd feel better if you waited for him before you went home."

We kissed her good night. I was very thankful that Corky had taken the time to talk to Mom. The two of them had always had a good relationship and could really communicate with each other. Throughout the years of our marriage, I would often joke that if Mom had been my age, I wouldn't have stood a chance.

Chapter 14

The next morning, the doctor told mom that there was nothing more they could do for her, so the best place to be was at home with her family. We left the hospital and drove to my house. Mom had really lost a lot of her strength and needed a lot of help getting out of the van. With my arm holding her tightly around her waist and her leaning on me, it took all her strength to walk into the house to the living room.

Just as she sat down on the couch, the phone rang. It was Judy, the home care nurse asking how things were going.

"We just got home from the hospital. Mom has agreed to stay with us for a few days. She's pretty weak. I'm just so glad she's willing to stay here."

She said, "I'm glad she's with you too. Did it take a lot of coaxing to get her to come to your place?"

"Not really. I think she realizes that she needs help now. She's going to go back to her house and stay with my brother when he gets here next week."

"That will make her very happy." She continued, "I only have a minute. I just called to let you know that I will be at your house this evening, and we can talk more then."

"That will be fine. See you later tonight."

I hung up and brought Mom a glass of juice. She tentatively took the glass in her hand, and with a worried look on her face she said, "I'm so afraid to eat or drink anything. I just can't handle getting sick anymore, but I am so hungry and thirsty."

I said, "I guess that's just going to be part of this blockage. There's so little moving into your bag now. Hopefully, we can find something that satisfies your hunger that won't come back up."

Mom said, "There has to be a way that I can keep down those high-calorie drinks I took before; I really want to gain weight. I am going to ask the nurse tonight when she comes over. She might have an idea on what might be good for that."

The day was almost gone. I noticed that it was nearing three o'clock, and I had to pick up the kids from school. They were very excited about Mom coming to stay with us again. I just hoped they wouldn't be too noisy and boisterous.

I knew that Mom hated being a burden to us. She had been a very independent person; she was always used to doing everything for everyone else, and now she was the one who was dependent. This was very hard on her.

ॐॐ

I parked in front of the school, just in time to see the kids run up the stairs to the van.

Winded, Tess said, "Is Grandma at our house yet?"

"Yes, she's having a nap."

"Oh good," Nigel said. "How is she feeling?"

"She's not too bad, I guess, except she's pretty tired and worn out."

"Poor Grandma," Nigel said. "If she hadn't smoked, she wouldn't be sick."

"Well, we'll never know. We had better hurry. Grandma's alone and I don't like to leave her for too long."

The kids had found a reason for Mom being sick, and they weren't going to give up on it. They had decided that it was the cigarettes. I never really told them otherwise. I didn't want to tell them that it could very well be genetic. I didn't want them to have to worry that something like this could happen to me—or to them, for that matter.

We arrived home to find Mom fast asleep on the couch. The kids sat at the kitchen table doing their homework as quietly as they could, and I prepared the evening meal.

Mom woke up a few hours later and joined us at the dinner table. She tentatively ate a small amount of food that consisted of vegetables and potatoes. After dinner, she retired to the family room to watch television with the kids until Judy, the home care nurse, arrived to get Mom ready for the night.

Judy had been Mom's nurse for the last nine months of her

illness, and in that time, they had developed a close friendship. Judy was a compassionate and caring nurse who was very efficient and very supportive. She always gave as much time as Mom needed without ever appearing rushed.

Once Mom was comfortable, Judy came out of her room to talk with me.

She began, "Carole, your mom really wants to go home to her own house."

I immediately felt annoyed. I had heard this so many times that I instantly got my back up. I was beginning to feel that somehow it was my fault that she couldn't go home by herself.

I bit my lip and said as nicely as I could, "I am well aware that she wants to go home, but it's obvious that she's in no shape to be alone right now."

She said, "Don't worry, Carole. I completely agree with you, but I have an idea. What if we set up a home support worker to take your mom to her place for the afternoon, three or four times a week? This would assure her safety while she is at her house."

"That's a great idea. But will the home support people do this?"

"I'll check first thing tomorrow, and hopefully we can set something up right away."

"That sounds good, but we'll only need this service for a week until Vern arrives."

"Okay, and I'll ask home support if they can continue the service after he goes back home." She looked at her watch and said, "I have to run. Someone will be here tomorrow morning, and I'll be back again tomorrow night."

I went into Mom's room and said, "Judy told me she is going to call home support to organize a weekly schedule to take you to your house for the day and bring you back here for the evenings. You can go to your place full time when Vern comes next week."

Mom said, "That's sounds good, but I'm not an invalid yet. I am going to get stronger. Judy told me to drink those high-calorie drinks from the drug store. She said they should give me energy, and then I'll be okay at my house alone."

"Yes, but please, just wait until Vern gets here, Okay?"

Aggravated, she said, "Fine. I'll wait until then, but I'm going home the minute he arrives."

I was getting so tired of fighting with her about her safety and always looking like the bad guy.

I curtly said, "That's fine with me too. I don't mind you being at home as long as you're not alone. So we are in sync."

Mom said, "Good. Now I'm going to go to sleep. I'm exhausted; it's been a long day."

I softened and said, "Let me get you comfortable for bed. Isn't this a switch Mom? The roles sure have changed."

"Yes, I guess they have, but it doesn't mean I like it."

I said, "Let me check your patch and make sure it's still sticking to your skin. You've got another twelve hours left. Are you feeling any pain?"

"Actually I do have some twinges in my lower stomach."

"Then we'd better put another patch on. There is no point in you waking up in the night in pain."

The pharmacist said that the analgesic patches could last for up to three days, but for Mom they lasted forty-eight hours at a time. Within five minutes of applying the patch to her back, she was relieved of her pain. There were no shots of morphine, no over-medicating, and no bruised skin. Most importantly, she continued to be mentally clear and alert.

As I was applying the patch to Mom's back, the kids came in to the room. They crawled onto the bed, and giving her kisses and hugs they told her how much they loved her. They said goodnight and left to get ready for bed.

I made sure Mom was comfortable for the night and then handed her the brass bell. I reminded her to ring it loudly if she needed me at any time throughout the night.

❧❧

The next morning while Mom was having breakfast and I was drinking my first coffee of the day, the phone rang. It was the home-support agency. They said that a schedule had been arranged for Mom for the week ahead. A homemaker had been assigned to drive Mom to her house three times a week on Monday, Wednesday, and Friday afternoons. The service would begin tomorrow. This was good news and made Mom very happy.

Mom finished her breakfast and announced that she had made arrangements to go play bingo with her friend Cathy at noon. I was surprised; I couldn't believe my ears. Did this woman ever stop?

I said, "How do you keep going? It's like you are the Ever-ready bunny!"

Mom chuckled, "I can't sit around doing nothing day after day; I need to get out a bit. I've been cooped up long enough."

"You are amazing, Mom; you're such a good example of how to live life to the fullest."

"Well," she stated flatly, "There's no point in sitting around moping."

Cathy had been Mom's best friend for at least thirty years. She was no spring chicken herself and had her own health problems. I worried about Cathy's ability to take care of Mom and wondered how she would cope if Mom had a problem.

Cathy arrived shortly after noon.

She said, "I'm going to take your mom to her house after bingo, so don't worry; I'll bring her back home around five tonight."

"You guys have a really good time. Call me if you need anything at all."

I watched them while they backed out of the driveway. I crossed my fingers and hoped that they would both be okay.

ର୍ଚ୍ଚ ଏହି

The week passed by quickly, with many of Mom's close friends dropping by to visit. She went to her house three days a week, where she would watch television lying comfortably on her couch. At the end of the day, she would come home from her visit and tell me that my couch hurt her back and her couch was perfect. I thought this was humorous. I knew she was just making a point that she should be at her house and not mine.

Mom had been at our house seven days when my brother arrived on my doorstep. Mom was napping, so I offered him a cup of tea and sat down at the kitchen table to have a chat.

He said, "So how are things going? Mom really wants to get home by the sounds of it."

"Yes, it's been so hard to get through to her that she can't stay by herself; she just doesn't get it. But there is something that's even more annoying than that. This morning she informed me that she wants all her furniture moved back to her house. I guess I have to get the moving company to move everything back to her place again."

Vern looked confused, "Why would she want you to do that? That's ridiculous. Don't bother moving anything yet."

"Well," I said, "Mom said that she's not coming back here; when you leave, she's staying at her house. I have to tell you that if I move her stuff back to her place, I will not be moving it back here again. I am so exasperated, not to mention exhausted. The way I feel right now, she can darn well go to the hospital when she finds out that she can't take care of herself."

"Wow, you sound so annoyed."

"I'm beyond annoyed. I have really had it. I can't keep moving her things back and forth, to and from my house. She didn't want to be here in the first place, and although she is way too sick and frail to stay alone, she refuses to accept that. I'm tired of it all. I feel I'm on call twenty-four hours a day, and now on top of everything, she wants me to move all her stuff back to her house; again."

Vern said, "Listen to me. Don't move her furniture back. There is no way she can be alone at her house; she is way too weak and frail. That much is obvious. She'll come to her senses when she sees that she can't do a lot of things on her own."

Sarcastically, I said, "Oh, really? And how is she going to find that out? You'll be there doing everything for her."

Vern sighed and said, "I won't do everything for her. I'll try to have her do most of the things that she would have to do if I weren't

113

there. Trust me, she'll figure it out." Vern took a deep breath and continued, "Look, you need a break, and that's why I'm here. Just relax and spend some time with Corky and the kids."

Changing the subject, he said, "Now, I brought some fresh salmon, oysters, and clams as I promised, so how about you following through with the offer to cook them for dinner tonight?"

"Damn," I said jokingly, "I knew I shouldn't have offered to do that. But you are going to have to help."

Just after five o'clock, we sat down to a feast of seafood. Mom had always loved fried oysters, but this time she hesitated to try them because she knew they would come right back up in an hour or so, and the thought of that wasn't too appealing. After some hesitation, she tried one anyway and really enjoyed it.

We were just finishing dinner and casually talking when Mom became fidgety and was itching to get home. We had barely finished eating when Vern and Mom left for her house.

I was relieved that Mom wasn't my responsibility for the next week, but at the same time I felt anxious being away from her. This feeling reminded me of when my kids were little. I needed a break then, too, but at the same time I didn't want to be away from them for very long. I had become attached to and protective of Mom in the same way. I had become in tune with her every need, and I hoped that Vern would be able to read the subtle signs when she was in distress; I knew she wouldn't complain to him unless things got really bad.

It scared me how much her illness had become such a big part of my life. I was tired of it all, but at the same time I was trapped in a situation that was impossible to get out of until she died. Even though I knew she was safe with my brother, it was hard to relax and stop worrying about her.

Vern phoned later that evening, "Well, Mom threw up dinner just as we got home, and now she's in bed sleeping. He hesitated and awkwardly said, "Mom emptied her colostomy bag before she went to bed. My God, I've never smelt anything like it. It's shocking, to tell you the truth."

"I know Vern. It's wicked. We have to open the doors and

windows after she changes it at our place. It seems to permeate throughout the whole house. I really don't know what would cause that smell."

I took a deep breath and said, "I have to tell you Vern, I hope that I die in a plane crash after a great holiday. There is no way that I want to die the way she is. It's so brutal."

Vern said, "I had no idea that you were dealing with all of this. You sure have had a lot on your plate, kid. I'm really glad I'm here to relieve you. I can see that this has been way too much for you."

"I'm glad you're here too, because I really need this break. I'm glad she's in your hands. It's a relief that I don't have the full responsibility of taking care of her for awhile."

Vern said, "When do you start school again?"

"I start tomorrow night, and I'm actually really looking forward to it. I'm going back into the real world, and I'm doing something other than being a caregiver."

Vern said, "Good. I'm glad you decided not to postpone finishing. Well, you just take it easy tonight. I'll give you a call tomorrow."

ॐ∻

The next few days were blissfully peaceful. I knew Mom was happy at her house, and this gave me uninterrupted time with Corky and the kids. I enjoyed my psychology class at the college, and even though it was going to be a lot of work, I knew it would be good for me. I felt like I was moving forward in my life. Vern called on a daily basis to give me updates on how Mom was doing. He told me that she had presented him with her list of projects that needed to be done around her house. She wanted him to put decorative white rocks around the junipers trees that had been planted along her driveway and paint the carport and the trim around her door white.

I couldn't understand why mundane things like that seemed so important to her when she had so little time left to live. I wanted to understand Mom's view on this, so I went to the bookstore and came upon a book called *Final Gifts[1]*. This book explains in great detail the process that a dying person goes through. I read about how important it was for the dying person to tie up all loose ends in their life. Everyone has things that are important to them, and if these are left undone, they find it very difficult to let go of this world and are unable to die in peace. This book helped me make sense of and understand what I thought was strange behavior. I was relieved to find out that it was very normal behavior for a person passing over.

ఇం ఈ

Four days into Vern's visit, he phoned me in a panic and asked me to come to the house as soon as possible because Mom was in crisis. I arrived at Mom's place to find her sitting on the couch slouched over a bucket. She was having a really rough time; she couldn't keep anything in her stomach, including water or juice. I phoned the doctor immediately. He said that she could go into the hospital or wait for him to come by her house tomorrow. I asked her what she wanted to do.

Mom said, "I dread going into that awful place. I will be alright, this isn't anything new. Tell him that I would really appreciate him coming by tomorrow; I'm sure I will be okay until then."

As I hung up the phone, she said, "This throwing up is really getting to me, I'm going to starve to death if I don't get something in me."

Vern and I looked at each other. We both had the same thought. Mom was probably going to starve to death before she would die from this cancer. The notion made me shudder. Neither of us knew what to say.

Vern broke the silence, "Mom, you're really having a rough time with this. When the doctor arrives tomorrow, we need to talk about what we should do after I leave. We have to increase your

---

[1] Maggie Callahan and Patricia Kelley, *Final Gifts: Understanding the Special Awareness, Needs and Communications of the Dying* (New York: Poseidon Press, 1992).

support system. Maybe we can get someone to stay overnight and homemakers can come and spend the day with you."

He went on, "Now, we don't mind setting this up for you, but quite honestly, I can't understand why you don't want to stay with your family." He paused and tentatively said, "You really should stay at Carole's house, Mom."

I added, "I agree, especially when you only have three weeks or a month left."

She looked over at me in shock, "What are you talking about! I have a lot longer than that. Dr. Morgan said that there could be months left."

I felt terrible about blurting that out. None of us had mentioned a time limit before, but I assumed that after the recent rupture of her intestine, she herself would have figured out that there was very little time left. Yet she was still fighting and denying that the cancer had beaten her. I couldn't believe it! I took a deep breath. I felt that the time had come to be honest.

I began, "Mom, there is no way that your intestine is going to heal. There is only a short time left, and we want you to be safe and around the people who love you. We certainly don't want you to spend your last month sitting all alone in your house."

"Carole, I want to be here. I'm used to being alone. I've done this for years, and I want to do it now, too. You guys are welcome to come and visit me as much as you like."

I sighed, "Okay Mom, I'm not going to argue with you. We'll leave it the way you want it for now. We can talk to the doctor tomorrow about this and see what he has to say."

I stood up and said, "I'm sorry guys, but I have to go. I have to pick the kids up from school."

Vern walked with me to my van, and said, "Man, she is so stubborn! There is no way that she can stay here by herself. She can barely walk anymore."

"I know, but she's determined to stay in her place. I will find out what services are available to make this happen. If this is what she wants, then we have to be sensitive to her request and comply with all her wishes. I will do this for Mom, but I sure don't understand her way of thinking at all."

Vern said, "Don't worry. When it comes to the crunch, I bet she won't stay here alone."

"I hope not, but we will have to wait and see. It's hard to believe, but she's still in so much denial."

When I arrived home, I phoned the homemakers to see what services they offered beyond the three days a week they were giving us now. I learned that to hire a person to stay overnight would cost three hundred dollars a night using a private firm. The alternative was that someone would come and tuck Mom in at night and return in the morning to check on her. This was subsidized by the government and was more reasonably priced at just fifty dollars a day.

ॐॐ

The next afternoon, I drove over to Mom's house to make sure I was there when the doctor came to visit. While waiting for Dr. Morgan to arrive, I gave Mom the information on the different services available to her.

She said, "Well, having someone staying overnight is out of the question. That's way too expensive."

I said, "What does it matter, if this is what you want to do? You have the money; so just spend it."

Mom ignored my suggestion and said, "I think I like the idea that someone would come and help me get ready for bed and then lock the doors. I think that would work for me. I know I'll be fine throughout the night, and the price sounds right."

"Okay Mom," I conceded, "let's just see how it goes."

The doorbell rang. It was Dr. Morgan. He came into the living room, sat on the couch beside Mom, and asked, "How are you feeling today?"

"Well, not too well. I've been throwing up all the time. Even juice won't stay down."

Dr. Morgan gravely said, "Since the recent rupture, your intestine is now completely blocked."

"Yes, I suspected that you would tell me that. I've accepted the fact that there is very little I can do about this. However, I also have another problem. My kids think I am going to die in three weeks. Is this true?"

Dr. Morgan said, "Anne, nobody can tell you when you are going to die. It could be two weeks, one month, or more. It is something that we can rarely estimate. I'm afraid that your vomiting is going to be almost impossible to stop because of the blockage in your intestine. The best that we can do is to prescribe you something for the nausea. It has to be given intravenously at the hospital or I can order the home care nurse to give it to you by injection."

Mom said, "I really don't want to go back to the hospital if I can help it. I'll take the injection."

Mom changed the subject and said, "There is one more thing; my kids don't want me to stay here alone after Vern leaves. I think I can handle staying here if I can get a little help."

Dr. Morgan said, "Anne it is your decision as to what you want to do and where you want to stay. I have no problem with you staying at your house with help."

After Dr. Morgan said goodbye to Mom, Vern and I walked with him to his car.

Vern said, "Dr. Morgan, I really wish you hadn't said that she was capable of staying here with help."

He replied, "You both have to give her the freedom to choose for herself. As I have told you many times, she is an adult and you have to be willing to let her make her own decisions. She has been independent for a long time, and she's not about to give that up without a struggle."

Vern said, "That's true. I know our motives are somewhat selfish, but it will be such a worry to think she is here alone in this state."

Dr. Morgan said, "If she gives in and stays at your house, it's an admission that her life is over, and she's not ready to do that yet."

We waved goodbye to Dr. Morgan and went back into the house. Vern was perturbed by what Dr. Morgan said. He was angry that he told Mom that she could stay here. He felt that the doctor was not being honest with her about how long she had to live.

I said, "I think he didn't give an exact time because he doesn't want to take away Mom's hope."

"But that's not honest; we all know there isn't any hope. It's so obvious that she's not going to last long. She's wasted away to nothing."

"Well, for some unknown reason, it's still not that obvious to Mom, so we have to try and understand her and be patient with her," I replied.

On the fifth day of Vern's visit, he made an appointment with a nutritionist at the hospital. He hoped to find a solution on how to help Mom absorb more nutrients into her system. He pressed fresh juices and made nutritious high-calorie drinks, but to no avail: nothing stayed down, and she continued to starve.

We didn't pressure Mom anymore about coming to stay at our house, but as the day of Vern's departure for Victoria came closer, she undecidedly said to me, "I might come and stay with you. I'm not sure yet."

࿉

Finally, the day of Vern's departure had arrived. As he was packing up his things and getting ready for his trip back home, Mom announced her decision about where she wanted to stay after Vern left.

She firmly said, "I've made up my mind. Everything is done here and the house is finally finished, so I'm ready to leave." She took a deep breath and said, "I think you're both right. I'm not so sure I would feel safe here alone. I have very little strength left, and, to be honest, I don't think I can handle taking care of myself anymore."

Vern and I looked at each other with relief. I was thankful that she had come to this decision on her own and had finally given up on the idea of staying at her house alone.

I began, "Mom, as difficult as this is, you are making the right decision. I know staying with us isn't what you want, but we will do our best to make it as easy and comfortable for you as we can. I know how attached you are to your couch because of its comfort. If you want, I can get the moving company to bring it to our house. That way you can watch television in the living room, like you do here."

"You don't have to. I'll be fine without it."

We packed Mom's personal items and clothing into a suitcase. Vern drove Mom to our house, and once Mom was settled and comfortable, he left for his long drive home.

❧

The kids arrived home from school later that day and were delighted to find that Mom had moved back to our house. Nigel gave Mom a big hug and asked, "Grandma, are you going to stay at our house for a long time? I promise I'll try to be really quiet so that I don't wake you up, and I won't make loud car and explosion noises either."

Mom laughed and said, "That's very nice of you Nigel, and yes, I'll be here for a while, I think."

Nigel said, "I am so glad you are here Grandma; you call me if you need anything."

He then went bounding off to watch one of his after-school television shows.

At that moment, I was so proud of Nigel. Even though he was only seven years old, he was willing to help out where he could. I had been worried about the kids being affected negatively by Mom's illness, but not so. They were getting invaluable lessons about empathy, love, compassion, and self sacrifice. It was important that the kids spend every precious moment possible with her. I knew then that we had done the right thing to have Mom here at home with us.

The days passed with the home care nurses and the homemakers coming and going. Mom was still getting sick. She'd eat a small amount of porridge in the morning and a broth soup for lunch and dinner. Nothing stayed down, not even ginger-ale or apple juice. Eventually, everything came back up again, and this was so frustrating for her. The hardest part was the nausea which was very overwhelming at times.

The nurse administered the anti-nausea drug to help with queasiness. She taught me how to inject the drug into the Heparin Lock that had been inserted in Mom's forearm. It was a plastic tube that was securely placed into her vein. This gave a port that we could administer different medications without giving her needles directly into her skin. It was completely pain free.

That morning after the home care nurse had attended to Mom, she asked me if we could talk in private about Mom's approaching death. She asked if I was going to keep her home to die. My first reaction was that of fear; the idea of watching her die in our house made me flinch. I was already at my wit's end, and I really didn't know how much more I could cope with. I had been taking Mom's illness one day at a time, and at that moment it was hard to think about the prospects of her dying, let alone dying in my spare bedroom. The notion of nursing her until death absolutely overwhelmed and terrified me.

I said, "To be honest, I don't know if I can handle Mom dying in our house. I've never seen a dead body before and I guess I really don't know if I can handle that." I took a deep breath and said, "More importantly, I worry that it might be hard on the kids."

"I completely understand. Don't feel guilty if you can't have her here. Not everyone can cope with nursing a dying person; it's a very tough job. I don't think you should make a decision right now. Take some time to think this through."

She handed me two pamphlets. One pamphlet was on the process of dying at home, and the other was on helping children cope with someone in the family who has a terminal illness.

I took a quick look at the pamphlets and said, "Nigel and Tess have been asking me about what was going to happen when she dies. I've been telling them that she will be free of her sick body and that she will still be with us, but it wouldn't be easy for us to see her. This seems to satisfy them for now; but we haven't lost her yet, so the reality hasn't really hit them."

She said, "Many of the families I have worked with over the years have feared death and didn't want to discuss the dying process, but you seem to have a positive philosophy about this important transition."

I said, "For many years I have thought of death as a transition or an evolution from one dimension or stage to another. However, now that I am facing Mom's death, I realize this concept looks great on paper, but not so much in reality. And even though I do think that we are much more than this physical body, the pain of losing her will be very real. I have a sense that having this belief system isn't going to protect me from experiencing the deep mourning and the loss of her, and it may not mean much when she finally passes over. I realize that it will be me that will be feeling the pain, not her."

"I too believe that we are more than the physical body, Carole, but you are right: It still doesn't make it any easier to lose the people we love. It takes a lot of courage to have someone pass over in your house, so like I said earlier, you certainly don't have to keep your mom here to die. You need to do what you feel is best for you and your family."

"Thanks for your kind advice. I certainly have a lot to think about, and I must admit that it scares the hell out of me."

After the nurse left, I went into Mom's room and found her sitting up on the bed. She still looked lovely even though she was so sick. She was wearing a white sweater and navy blue pants. Her clothes these days were casual and comfortable: no more designer suits and high-heeled shoes that she had worn for many years.

I sat down beside her and said, "You look nice Mom. Your skin is still so beautiful."

Mom laughed and said, "That's very nice of you to say, but unfortunately when I look at myself in the mirror, I wonder who that person is."

"Well, you look like my beautiful Mom, and that will never change."

Mom patted my cheek and then asked, "I would like to get out of this bedroom for awhile; can you help me to the living room?"

"Sure. I am so glad you want to get out of this room."

I put my arm around her waist and held her arm while she found her balance. She shuffled her feet slowly forward and leaned on me for support. We walked bit by bit into the living room, finally making it to the couch; she sat down sighing with relief that she had made it.

She breathed, "Boy, that's exhausting!"

I said, "I've made a pot of tea. I will bring us a cup and then we can talk."

As we were sipping our tea, Mom began, "I know I don't have much time left. I know I'm dying, and I accept that there's not much I can do about it anymore."

She paused, shaking her head. "I just can't get past the regret of working too long. I had planned to take a cruise on a ship, just like the first time I came to Canada on the Queen Mary, you know, just for old time's sake. I had planned to take my grandchildren to Disneyland. She took a deep breath and said, "I so foolishly thought I had lots of time."

She stared quietly out the window. I took a sip of tea. What could I say? I wanted so much to take all her pain away, to change everything that had happened to her in the last year, but I knew that was impossible. I too had to resign myself to her approaching death.

A few moments went by when I said, "Mom, it's going to be alright. I believe you move on to a new dimension and a new life, so to speak."

Mom looked at me skeptically and laughed, and said, "What happens if there is nothing after death and this is all there is? I really don't know what to believe. I just know I have to face my death alone."

"Mom, don't you remember your near-death experience in the Intensive Care Unit last December? You said you were embraced in golden light. And remember when Leif said that he'd be here for you when you were ready to leave the next time?"

She shook her head slightly and said, "Carole, so much of that has faded. I do remember it, but it seems like a dream now."

I asked, "Doesn't it give you a bit of hope that you won't be alone and that there is something more out there for you?"

"It's hard for me to find any hope about anything right now. I have no future. It's a strange feeling: it's as if I'm on the edge of a cliff with nothing before me."

"Well like I said before, when you finally leave your body, you're going to say 'That daughter of mine was right. This is fantastic! I was never that body anyway.'"

Mom laughed heartily, "Boy, you do have a good imagination!"

It was surprising how both of us could laugh over this intense subject about her approaching death.

This was the second conversation we had about life after death. I was relieved that her impending death was finally out in the open, and that now she could really discuss her pain, fears, and disappointments.

At this point, Mom was tired and wanted to relax. I turned the television on and within minutes she was fast asleep.

I tiptoed out of the room and phoned Vern and Sandy. "Mom is really going downhill fast. Now that she's accepting that she's not going to live much longer, I don't think she's going to be around for long. I'd be surprised if she lasts two more weeks."

Sandy said, "Then we're coming this Friday. I have to see your mom again. I would be so sad if I couldn't spend a little more time with her. We'll come and give you a break and take Anne over to her house while we are visiting."

"I am so happy to hear that. I don't think you guys will regret coming. We'll see you in a couple of days."

The homemaker arrived Friday morning to give Mom a bath, do her hair, and help her get ready for Vern and Sandy's visit. Mom needed a lot of assistance to get into the bathtub. We lifted her legs over the edge of the tub one leg at a time and lowered her carefully into the water, but it was well worth the effort because she enjoyed bathing so much.

Once she was lying safely in the warm water, she blissfully said, "Oh this is heavenly. The heat is so soothing on my aching bones."

This had been one of her favorite past-times before she became ill. Over the years, there had been many evenings when I would phone to have a chat and she would be soaking in the bathtub, reading a book.

❧❦

Vern and Sandy arrived that afternoon to take Mom to her house. Mom was all packed and excited to be going back to her place to spend the weekend. We went over all the details regarding the anti-nausea drug and the pain medication before everyone left.

On the way to the car, Vern said, "Don't worry; Mom will be fine with us. We'll phone you if there are any problems at all."

"I know that she's in good hands with the two of you."

Vern gave me a hug and assured me, "We can handle this just fine. You definitely need a break, and you've got your family to think of." Shaking his head, he said, "I just can't believe how much you have had to deal with. I feel so bad that I can't be here all the time to help you."

"Thanks, Vern, but I'm okay—and don't worry about the family. Mom takes precedence right now. And yes, the kids have had to sacrifice some things for their Grandma, but at the same time, they also want me to take care of her. They've been very helpful and accepting through all of this."

Vern said, "I know, but you still need to spend some time on your own, so don't worry about anything."

Before we got Mom settled in the car, I gave her a hug and said, "Have a great time at your house. I'm so glad you get to be at your place again. We'll come over and see you tomorrow."

"All right sweetie. See you tomorrow."

Chapter 15

It was Saturday, October 24, and it was my forty-first birthday. First thing that morning, Mom phoned me to wish me a very happy birthday.

I asked her, "So how does it feel to wake up in your house?"

"Oh, it's so great to be here. I had a really good sleep. I really like being around all my things, and today I'm going to putter around and look at everything."

"That sounds like a nice thing to do. Maybe pull out your photo albums, and look at some of your old pictures."

"That's a thought; I think I will. Vern wants to talk to you. I'll see you later today."

There was a pause, and then Vern came on the phone and said, "Happy birthday, kiddo. It's hard to believe you are so old. But you don't look a day over forty."

"Very funny, Vern: Just remember pal, I will always be younger than you, and I don't intend to let you ever forget it."

Vern laughed and asked, "Do you want to go out to dinner tonight and celebrate?"

"That would be fun, but do you think Mom can handle sitting in a restaurant?"

"Mom said she would love to come, but she doesn't feel up to it. We'll just go for an hour or two by ourselves."

"I don't think we should leave her alone for that length of time. What if she needs something? She's so weak, I don't think that she will be able to make it to the bathroom on her own without help."

"Look, she really wants us to go for your birthday dinner. She said that she will rest on the couch and watch television."

"Okay, but let's have an early dinner. I'll make a reservation at The Lodge. We'll come to the house around four o'clock." I said.

"Perfect, see you then."

෪෴

We arrived at Mom's place just after four o'clock. Mom was comfortably stretched out on her couch, watching television. When I walked into the room, she gave me a big smile, cheerfully wished me a very happy birthday, and handed me a birthday card.

I was surprised that she had a card for me.

"Oh thank you! But how did you get this card." I asked.

She smirked and said, "Oh, I have my ways." And with a twinkle in her eye she said, "Well the truth is, Sandy went into town and bought it last night."

I opened the card and found a check. Mom was always so generous. In the past, we'd had a yearly birthday tradition where we went shopping for clothes and had a leisurely lunch, but this year that was going to be impossible.

"Thanks Mom. You're always so good to me. I've been thinking about dinner, why don't we order take-out and eat here so we can all be together."

Mom said, "No, that's okay. I can't eat much anyway. I'll be fine; you guys go and have a nice dinner. I'm enjoying myself, and a little time alone would be nice."

"Well, alright, but we won't be long. Call us for anything at all."

We arrived at the restaurant around five o'clock. It was nice to have a glass of wine and a dinner that I didn't have to cook.

Tess and Nigel loved being with Uncle Vern and Aunt Sandy; they had a way of making the kids feel special. My brother loved joking around with them, and he never stopped with the one liners.

As they were talking and laughing, I found myself drifting away into my thoughts. If Mom hadn't become ill, Vern and I would still be quite distant and semi-formal with each other. It was healing to have spent the last eight months talking about the many misunderstandings we had about each other over the years. It was true: stressful events really did bring people together.

My mind returned to our table and the ongoing conversation around me.

I interrupted them and said, "Hey guys, we need to get back to Mom. We've been gone long enough."

಄•಄

We walked into Mom's house to find that she wasn't on the couch in the living room where we had left her. Perplexed, I called out her name. There was no answer. I quickly walked down the hallway to see if she was in her bedroom. I was stunned at what I saw. Mom was lying on the bed, half-dressed and shivering. I looked around the room and saw four soiled towels strewn on the floor.

I rushed into the room and gasped, "Oh my God! What has happened Mom? Are you alright?"

She said weakly, "I tried to get up from the couch to walk to the bathroom because my colostomy bag began leaking. I got the bag undone, but I was too weak to stand up without hanging on to something. My hands have no strength, and I couldn't peel the sticker off the new flange to put on my bag. All I could do was get to the bed and lie down, but then I couldn't get myself off the bed."

I felt awful. We never should have gone out to dinner and left her alone. I asked Sandy to phone the home care nurse to come as quickly as possible. Mom was in a real mess. She was shivering from being so cold; she hadn't even had the strength to pull the covers over herself.

She said in shame, "I'm such a burden; I'm so useless. I can't do anything anymore. I've lost all my strength." Humiliated, she said, "I'm so embarrassed!" She began to cry and said over and over, "I'm so sorry, I'm so sorry."

"Don't do this to yourself, Mom. You can't help what's happened to you. You shouldn't be sorry. You're sick, and you need us to help you; don't feel embarrassed. It's okay."

I had never changed her colostomy bag before. The nurse had always managed to do it if Mom couldn't. I asked Mom to tell me how it worked. She told me to cut the hole in the flange and put it over the opening and then attach the bag. I did this the best that I could.

I said, "I don't know if this is done very well, but at least you're

129

not leaking all over the place. When the nurse comes, she can change it if she wants. But in the meantime let's get you into the bathtub."

After Mom's bath, Sandy and I helped her out of the tub. As we were drying her, I noticed that her body was skin and bone; there wasn't any flesh left at all, not even on her buttocks. The only area that had any kind of fullness was the large tumor protruding from her abdomen.

I said, "Let's get some pajamas on you and get you warm and comfortable for the night."

Mom said, "I'm exhausted; I think I will go to sleep now."

I asked, "Do you want your sleeping pill?"

"Yes, please. I will rest until the nurse comes, and then I will go to sleep after she's gone."

We tucked her, along with a hot water bottle, into clean bedding and covered her with her big down quilt. She was still shivering. She was so frail, defenseless, and vulnerable. It broke my heart to see Mom in this terrible state.

Smiling slightly, Mom thanked us profusely.

This was devastating for Mom; she was completely at the mercy of everyone around her. This ordeal was very difficult for her, yet she handled this adversity with so much composure and dignity.

Just as we were opening the doors to air out the house, the nurse arrived. She immediately went into Mom's room and checked the colostomy bag to make sure it was secure, and then with everything in order, she walked back into to the living room to discuss what had just happened.

She said, "I see that you guys had a bit of excitement here tonight."

Sandy answered, "We were in a bit of a panic, to say the least. Mom was in pretty bad shape when we arrived home. We didn't realize how weak she really was, and if we'd been more observant, we wouldn't have left her alone this evening."

The nurse replied, "Yes, I can see that she's lost most of her strength. It's important that she's watched closely now. But, at the moment, I think everything is under control. Is there anything more I can do for you guys?"

Vern said, "No, I think we can handle it from here."

The nurse replied, "Okay. A nurse will be around first thing tomorrow morning."

かぶ

On the way home, Corky spoke about his concerns about Mom. "I can't believe how little strength Anne has left. She was even too weak to pick up the phone beside her bed to call for help. I didn't realize she was that frail."

"I had no idea it was that bad either," I admitted.

Corky replied, "You know, even though Anne has admitted that she can't stay alone anymore, I think she still had hopes that she could be somewhat independent; this has confirmed that there is no possible way that she can be left alone at all."

I agreed, "Yes, it's been tough for her to give up her independence. I know that I would absolutely hate people telling me what to do and having to depend on others for everything I needed."

I paused, "I think one of the things that bother her is that her illness has put me in the position of having to take care of her. And when I think about that, I do understand. I wouldn't want to burden my kids, either. I know I would feel really bad about that."

He said, "I think most of us would feel that way. So let's do our best to alleviate some of that guilt. Let's reinforce the fact that we want to have her with us for as long as she wants to stay. The hospital would be a terrible place for her right now."

I squeezed Corky's hand in gratitude. "Thank you, I appreciate all the support you're giving both of us. I honestly don't know what I would do without you." I paused, "But in the meantime, I guess we will have to wait and see what she wants to do, and make sure it is her decision and not ours."

I phoned Mom's house the next morning and Sandy answered.

I asked, "So how are you all doing today? How is Mom?"

"You know, considering what happened last night, Mom has

recuperated quite well. She had a good night's sleep and was her cheerful self this morning."

I could hear sadness in her voice when she said, "We feel so bad that we can't stay any longer to help you. I hate that we have to leave tomorrow. We'll bring Mom back to your place in the morning, and maybe we can have a cup of coffee together before we head out."

"Okay, I'll have the coffee on. I hope Mom's not going to be too sad about leaving her place again."

Sandy replied, "I don't think so. After last night, I think she realizes that she can't stay here alone. To tell you the truth, Carole, I don't think she even wants to be by herself anymore. Last night's event was pretty scary for her. I think she's beginning to accept her frailty and dependence on other people."

"I hope you're right."

Sandy said, "Mom's having a nap right now. I'll tell her you called. I am sure she will call you when she wakes up. If I don't talk to you before, we'll see you tomorrow morning around nine-thirty."

ॐ⊸ॐ

Mom, Vern, and Sandy arrived at our house at ten the next morning. Vern helped Mom out of the car, but she didn't want help walking to the house. She still wanted to walk by herself. It was painful to watch. I could see that it was taking every ounce of her strength and willpower to get through the back door and to a chair in the kitchen.

By the time she sat down, she was completely worn out, "I'm sorry guys, but I can't visit. I am exhausted, and I have to lie down."

We helped her to bed and went back into the kitchen to have coffee.

Vern said, "Boy, she's in rough shape. I can see that there isn't much time left now. I can't see her lasting even another week. I'm so glad she's with you Carole. He paused and then said, "I've been thinking about you keeping Mom here at the house to die, and to be honest, I really don't think you should do it. It's going to be too hard on you."

I said, "It's definitely going to be difficult, and I don't know what decision I'll make. I feel supported when you guys are here helping, but now that you are leaving, I feel the load on my shoulders again. I'm not meaning to make you feel guilty when I say this, but if you lived in Vernon, I could maybe keep her at home until the end. But being alone, I don't know if I can manage it."

Vern sighed, "I feel bad that I can't be here to help you, but I have to work. However, there is another option that Sandy and I have talked about. We could take Mom home to Victoria and have her at our house."

"How are you going to get her there?" I pointed out, "There is no way she could stand the drive."

"We were thinking of putting her on the plane."

"Vern, no offense or anything but that really won't work. There is no way she could handle a plane flight. And what about her friends who come to visit her? If she's in Victoria, she won't be near the people she cares about other than you guys."

I went on, "And what happens when she's close to death?"

Vern said, "We'll take her to the hospital and stay with her."

"Thanks Vern, but she would be very upset if we did that. Don't worry. I know you're doing this to relieve me of all this stress, but the truth of the matter is—as selfish as it sounds—I couldn't be away from her and have her die without being able to say goodbye. Thanks for trying to help me out. I really appreciate it, but I have to finish what has been started."

Then with a humorous tone, I said, "I'll tell you what Vern, I get to call you anytime and you have to listen to me whine and snivel and do everything you can to make me feel better."

We all laughed, and he said, "Okay, it's a deal." Vern stood up and said, "Well Sandy, we have a seven-hour drive ahead of us, we'd better head out."

This was the last time Sandy saw Mom while Mom was still alive, and I think they both had that knowing as they said their goodbyes.

ॐॐ

Shortly after Vern and Sandy left, I began cleaning up the kitchen. As I was loading the dishwasher, the phone rang. It was my friend Sarah.

"How are you holding up, and how is your mom?"

"Oh, I am hanging in there, but Mom isn't doing that great. I can see a big change in her now. I thought that she would spend more time in the living area with us, but she'd rather stay in her bed most of the time. I have to say, it's so hard to see her losing ground."

Sarah said, "I know what you're going through. I remember when my mom had cancer, and in the end stages, it spread to her brain. It was so difficult seeing her deteriorate before my eyes."

"That would be so heartbreaking Sarah."

"It was, but you are lucky, you know. At least you can communicate with your mom. I couldn't with mine; the cancer destroyed her memory. She would get things mixed up: She couldn't remember her grandchildren's names or how many she had, those sorts of things." She paused, "I think one of the most difficult times was when I went to see her one day, and she didn't recognize me."

She cleared her throat and went on, "I still miss her, especially when the kids have something special happening in their lives and I want to tell her about it. I don't think you ever forget or really get over losing your mother."

I asked, "I wonder why people have to suffer so much."

"I don't know. It doesn't seem fair. My mom was such a good person and to suffer like that just didn't seem right. You hang in there, Carole. I know what a tough time you're having, and I want you to call me anytime. I'm here if you need me."

"Thank you, I really appreciate that. It's nice to be able to count on you; I might take you up on your offer one of these days, especially when I'm having a nervous breakdown!"

"You'll get through this, Carole. I'll bring Tess and Nigel home after school today."

"That would be a great help. Thanks Sarah, see you later this afternoon."

I hung up the phone.

I was warmed by my friends who phoned on a daily basis to check on how things were going. They were always willing to lend a helping hand. Over the last few weeks, they had shown up unexpectedly at my door to drop off home-made casseroles, cookies, and cakes, along with an encouraging word.

I looked at the clock; it was close to lunchtime. I thought I had better check on Mom and see if she wanted something to drink.

I went into her room and asked, "What would you like to have for lunch, Mom?"

She thought for a moment and said, "How about that chicken broth in a cup? Do you have any left?"

"Yes I do, and I also have beef in a cup for later. At least it's a bit of a change."

I brought Mom a warm cup of chicken broth. She had a hard time lifting the cup to her lips, but with a lot of effort and shaking hands, she managed to take a drink. She enjoyed the broth so much that she sighed noisily after each sip.

As I watched Mom drink her soup, I found myself thinking about what a terrible thing it was to have to give up one of life's most cherished pleasures—eating. I realized at that moment that Mom was slowly starving to death. It wasn't the cancer that would ultimately kill her; it would eventually be the lack of nutrition.

Mom said, "Now, let's see if the soup will stay down this time."

"Well let's think positively, but just in case, here's a bowl on the side dresser, if you feel sick."

We both knew that she would be sick within the next half an hour or so, but we always hoped that it wouldn't happen.

I changed the subject. "We brought your books from your house, if you feel like reading."

"I love reading and I really miss it, but I'm having a hard time concentrating. I don't know why, but I can't seem to finish even one page. I read a few lines and I lose interest."

"It might be your medication. I can see how it could affect your concentration."

"Maybe, but I can't really blame it all on the medication. When

I think back, I've been like this ever since I had my operation last December."

"That's odd isn't it? I wonder why that is?"

"I don't know. Anyway, I'll try again now. I really do hope I can read today; but if I can't, I'll have a nap instead."

"Okay Mom, I'll leave you to it. Give me a shout if you need anything."

༄ ༅

That evening, the home care nurse arrived to change Mom's colostomy bag. This was always a major event for our family because the smell was unbearable. It must have been so humiliating and exasperating for Mom, but she never said anything and neither did we.

Once this ordeal was over and Mom was comfortable for the night, the nurse came out of the room and asked if she could talk with me for a short time.

She began, "I can see changes happening to your mom almost daily now. She is rapidly deteriorating, and from what I can tell, I don't think there is a lot of time left. She paused, reached out for my hand, and said, "I just want you to know that your mom has to be one of the nicest patients we've had. We feel very privileged to be able to care for her."

I was so touched and replied, "What a kind thing to say. I've been really fortunate to have her for a mom. I know I say that all the time, but I really mean it."

"You really are making her last days as comfortable as they can be. Many people in her condition are in the hospital all alone, waiting to die. She's lucky to be in such a loving environment surrounded by such a caring family."

"Well, I haven't always been the best daughter. I put her through so much when I was in my late teens and early twenties. I've often felt guilty about my backpacking trip I took to Europe when I was twenty. Mom thought I was going to visit her family in England and Scotland. I remember how excited she was that I was going to meet her two sisters and extended family. She assumed I would be gone for two or three months at the most.

"Around the two-month mark, I decided to travel overland through Turkey and the Middle East on my way to India. Mom had no idea I was in the Middle East until I wrote her a letter informing her that I was in Kabul, Afghanistan, waiting to travel to India."

I paused, "Of course I had to pick the worst time to go. The Pakistan/Indian war was full blown at the time. I remember seeing big headlines on a *Time* magazine cover: 'People are stranded in India; no one can get in or out of India'. But that didn't stop me or my travel companions in any way. We were told that the border from Pakistan into India was open every Tuesday morning, and that it was easy to get into India on that particular day. I was very naïve, and I actually believed that it was safe to cross over the border on foot. I actually believed that the war stopped every Tuesday morning. Of course now I shake my head and think how foolish that was. It was a very scary day for me; I had no concept of war and what that really meant. I am so lucky that nothing happened to me and that I got through the border without any complications.

"It never entered my mind to consider Mom's feelings. I swear that when I got home a year later, she looked ten years older. But the worst of it all was that I didn't go to England or Scotland; I never met any of her family. I was so self-absorbed in those days. I put her and her needs on the back burner; I was always too busy doing my own thing. I know that's pretty common, but I still feel bad about it, especially now."

The home care nurse said, "I think in times like these, we look back and think of all the things we should or could have done better; that is human nature. I don't think we ever feel that we've done enough."

"Isn't that the truth?"

The nurse said, "I'm going to look in on your mom one more time, and then I had better get on to my next patient."

While she was in Mom's room, I thought about all the support I was receiving from the home care nursing staff and how it would have been impossible to have done this without their help. Not only did they care for Mom, they lifted my spirits by giving me the opportunity to express my regrets, fears and sadness.

The nurse came back and said Mom was asleep. Another nurse would be at the house around eleven o'clock the following day.

Chapter 16

It was the end of October. I drove the kids to school and returned home to help Mom get dressed and ready for the day. As she was dressing, she began having twinges of pain in her abdomen, so I quickly added another patch to her back. I was amazed at the speedy relief these patches always gave her. Within minutes the pain subsided.

Mom was really hungry and asked if she could have porridge in the dining room. I helped seat her at the table, and she ate the whole bowl heartily. "Boy, I was really hungry. Thank you that really hit the spot."

Then sheepishly she said, "But I imagine that I will be seeing it all again soon."

I consoled her, "I know, Mom, but at least you got to eat something."

I changed the subject and said, "Tom and Barney phoned last night, just after you went to bed. They want to come and visit you this afternoon. Do you feel up to it?"

"Sure. It will be nice to see them. My hair is a real mess, though. Can you do something with it?"

"Sure, I can use the curling iron and you'll be a brand new woman."

"Wouldn't that be nice? It would take a miracle for that to happen," Mom joked.

With Mom's hair styled and face made up, she looked amazingly well, considering how ill she was. Tom and Barney had been close friends of Mom for forty years. They had been very good to her, especially over the last twenty years when she had managed one of their many bookstores.

They arrived at the house in the early afternoon for their visit. Mom seemed to be really enjoying herself when out of the blue, Mom was overwhelmed with fatigued and needed to lie down. Tom and

Barney understood and told her that they would come back and see her again soon.

Standing at the door, Barney said to me, "Carole, I'm so sorry this is happening. I just don't understand any of this. I find myself thinking about Anne all the time, and all I can say to myself is that I can't believe it. This simply doesn't seem right, especially since she has just retired. This should have been the good times for her."

"I know, Barney. We're having a hard time believing it too. Thank you for your support and love. Please come and visit Mom anytime. You are always welcome."

Tom remarked, "Thanks Carole, but your big dog sure isn't welcoming. She growls at us.

I said, "I am so sorry about that. I will put Kira in the back yard next time you come. I should have thought to do that."

He added, "Well, she sure is beautiful. What kind of dog is she?"

"She's an Akita, a breed from Japan." I continued, "She's become overly protective since Mom's been staying with us. I've never seen her act like this in the five years we've had her. She growls and barks at everyone who comes through the door.

"When the nurse arrives, Kira will bark and run over to Mom's door and lie down across the threshold, growling and not letting the nurse in to Mom's room. I tell Kira to move, and with a lot of resistance she'll finally leave, but she continues to howl as she walks away, with her head down and her tail between her legs."

Chuckling, I added, "It's quite comical actually. I have no doubt that she knows that Mom is vulnerable, so Kira has elected herself as Mom's sentinel."

Tom laughed and said, "Well you've got yourself a good dog there. Tell your mom I'll phone tomorrow."

I had to go to my first psychology class of the semester that night, so Corky was left in charge of Mom and the kids. The home care nurse came and went, and the rest of the evening went by uneventfully.

I awoke early the next morning. I made coffee and then went into Mom's room to see if she was awake. I found her in an extremely agitated state and very upset.

Mortified, she said, "Carole, I urinated all over the bed in the night. I should have gone to the bathroom before I went to sleep last night, but I forgot."

"Oh Mom, that's my fault. I should have thought of it before I left for my class. I should have reminded Corky about this."

Angrily she said, "I can't believe I did this. I can't stand this anymore; I've become so useless and so helpless. I can't even control my bladder anymore!"

"Mom, don't worry; I'm sure this is just a one-time thing. We'll just have to be more careful in the future. It's been at least twelve hours since you've gone to the bathroom, not to mention the medication you're taking makes you sleep more soundly. Come on, I'll get you into the bathtub. That'll make you feel better."

I felt so sorry for Mom. She was so humiliated by what had happened. It was like being a child again, and it was too much for her to handle.

As Mom relaxed in the warm water, I reassured her again that it was no big deal that she was incontinent. But as I said these words, I realized they rang untrue because inside, I was panicking.

I silently worried, Oh God, how am I going to cope with incontinence?

This was overwhelming for me. I'm far from being a nurse, and this wasn't something I could handle very well. How was I going to be able to deal with this?

I helped Mom out of the tub, got her dressed, and then settled her on the couch in the living room. She was in bad shape—both emotionally and physically—and looked so lost and scared.

I held her hand and said, "Mom, it's all right. I'll get a bathroom chair that we can leave at the side of the bed."

"Carole, that's great, except I don't have the strength to get out of bed by myself anymore. I can hardly adjust my hips without someone moving me. You can't handle this anymore, sweetheart; this is just too much for you."

I knew she was right. I was stressed to the maximum—emotionally depleted and exhausted—but I couldn't tell her that, so I lied and said, "Mom, I'm fine. I can handle it, really."

She adamantly said, "No you can't; I want to go back to the hospital. I'll feel better there."

"Mom, you hate the hospital. How could you want to go back there?"

"Really; I'll feel better there because if I have any accidents, they're equipped to handle the mess."

At that moment, the doorbell rang. I said, "Hang on Mom, someone's at the door."

It was Judy, Mom's favorite nurse from home care. She walked into the living room, sat down beside Mom, and reached for her hand. "Anne, are you alright? Carole told me you were incontinent in the night."

Mom self-consciously said, "Yes, and I am so embarrassed."

"You shouldn't feel badly about this; it can happen to anyone."

To my surprise, Mom said with conviction, "Judy, I want to go to the hospital. I would feel much better there because they can handle any problems that I might have."

Judy hesitated and then said, "Well if you'll feel better at the hospital, then that is where you should be. But are you sure this is where you want to go?"

"Yes, I'm sure."

Judy turned to me and said, "I'm going to call the ambulance to come and take your mom to the hospital."

I was upset. I didn't want Mom to die in a cold hospital, but what could I do? She was very adamant as to what she wanted, and to be honest, part of me was relieved as I wasn't sure I could handle any more of this stress. I was a big bag of mixed emotions.

I walked to the kitchen with Judy while she called the ambulance.

Judy looked at me compassionately and said, "It's okay, Carole. Sometimes people want to die in the hospital. Maybe your mom doesn't want to die here because she feels it would be too hard on you. Believe it or not, some people feel safer in a hospital setting."

I said, "I can't imagine that, but I guess it's important to let her make that decision. I didn't expect this to happen, but I admit I do feel somewhat relieved. I'm not very good at handling someone else's body fluids. I am so torn. I hate to see her in the hospital in such a sterile, lonely environment to die, yet I don't know if I can handle having her here either."

Judy gave me a hug. "I know this is really hard for you. You've come a long way with this. I can understand that you want to try and finish it, but if your mom feels better in the hospital, then that is where she should be."

"Yes, I know your right."

Judy said, "Let's get the bed cleaned up while we're waiting for the ambulance."

After we started the wash, I walked back into the living room to talk with Mom. She looked so sad, and I could sense her despair.

"How are you doing Mom?"

Looking down at her folded hands, she whispered, "I'm okay I guess."

Then she looked up at me with her sad brown eyes and said, "Carole, I hope you understand. It's not that I don't like it here. You've been wonderful, but I have too many physical problems. I need to be lifted on a regular basis, and now I've become incontinent; all of this will be too hard on you."

With a lump in my throat I said, "I think I can handle this Mom, but I'm okay with whatever decision you make. I'm so sorry this is happening to you. I wish I could take all this pain away and make you well again."

"I know. I do too. But we can't, so we have to accept things as they are and make the best of them."

I smiled and said, "You are so amazing Mom, you always see the positive side to every situation."

At that moment, I wondered what was really going on in her mind. She must have felt so afraid, so helpless, but still she wouldn't show me her real feelings. I knew that she was putting me first; she didn't want to burden me.

The ambulance arrived about half an hour later. Two men lifted Mom on a stretcher and covered her with a grey wool blanket. At that moment, she looked like a small child: She was so tiny and vulnerable.

"Mom, I'll pack a bag with all your things and I'll be right along behind you. I'll meet you at the hospital within the hour."

"Alright honey. I'll see you later, and don't worry. I'll be fine."

"I know you will Mom. See you soon."

&-&

After the ambulance left, I slumped wearily into a chair and broke down and cried. They were tears of frustration amidst overwhelming feelings of sadness and despair. How much longer was she going to suffer? How much longer did we have to watch her waste away to nothing? Mom's life force was being sucked out of her bit by bit. It all seemed so heartless and so cruel.

I was numb with the realization that this was probably going to be it. This was where Mom was going to die, and I just had to wait until it was all over. The words, "What will I do without her?" kept reverberating in my mind.

I got up, wiped my tears, went into the bedroom, and packed Mom's personal items—sleeping pills, clothes and slippers—and drove to the hospital. I found Mom on the second floor, in a private room across the hall from the nurses' station. She was sitting on her bed drinking apple juice.

"Hi, Mom. You look comfortable."

"Yes, I feel good. I won't have to wake you up and disturb you anymore. I feel quite safe here."

"I'm glad Mom, but you haven't disturbed me. I really liked having you at our house."

"I know, but this makes it easier for everyone. I'm a lot of work now, and I feel better that you don't have to do so much."

"Well if you decide that you want to come home, the door is always open."

"I know, love, but this is fine."

Suddenly Mom panicked. "Oh no, I think the apple juice is going to come back up!"

Mom said that in the nick of time, just before she threw up in the pan I handed her. I was amazed at how much liquid could come up from such a small glass of juice. I handed her a fresh pan and emptied the first one while she was heaving. I emptied the second pan and gave her another clean one.

She always became so exhausted after these bouts of vomiting. The heaving was beyond her control; she just had to let it take its course until her stomach was empty.

Mom laid her head back on the pillow and said, "I'm exhausted. I think I'm going to have a nap."

"That's a good idea. I'm going to pick up the kids from school in a few minutes and make dinner, and then I'll come back and see you this evening."

Dinner time at our house was not a happy occasion. I had a very heavy heart, and the kids were disappointed that Grandma wasn't staying at our house anymore. I had so many mixed emotions about her being in the hospital. The pressure was off, but I really missed her.

As we were clearing the dinner table, Corky said, "You know, she probably won't be coming out of the hospital again. She's really deteriorated this last week. He paused and gently said, "I feel it could be just a matter of days now."

I answered, "I know. I just hate this. How much longer is she going to hang on? I don't want her to die, but I don't want her to suffer like this anymore, either. Part of me just wishes she would give up and let go, but then there is a bigger part that just doesn't want to let her go."

"I know. I feel the same way, but she could let go really soon and it's not going to be easy for you."

"I know," I sighed. "We have so little time left with her, and yet

I find myself wishing all of this torment was over. I feel guilty when I get these feelings; I guess it's just so overwhelming. I know the outcome. I know what's going to happen, and I guess I just want to get that part over with. Yet, I dread it terribly."

Corky gave me a hug and said, "We'll get through this. You had better get to the hospital, I will finish up here. Don't worry about the kids; I will put them to bed."

⧆⧆

I arrived at the hospital close to seven that evening. I found Mom in a good mood.

I asked, "Are the nurses checking on you regularly? Are they checking the pain patches?"

"Yes, they've been great. They put another patch on this afternoon." Changing the subject, she said, "How are the kids?"

"They're fine, except they really miss you. I asked them if they wanted to come and visit you tonight, but they really have a hard time coming to the hospital, Mom."

"I understand. This is no place for kids because it's so boring for them."

"It's not that they get bored; it's all the sick people and the smell of the hospital that bother them. They were really sad that you weren't at home after school. Tess is pretty upset. She hides her feelings a lot of the time, but when she's tired and crawls into bed at night, it pours out of her. She doesn't think it's fair that you're sick."

Mom looked down at her tissue and said, "I love those kids so much. There were so many things I wanted to do with you and the kids, but," she shrugged her shoulders, "I got sick and that put an end to all my dreams."

I hugged Mom and said, "All of this has been so hard on you, and yet you have been so calm and in many ways so positive throughout this ordeal."

"There is no point in doing it any other way. I only have a short time left, so I might as well be as happy as I can be."

By this time, Mom looked really tired.

I offered, "Why don't I help you get ready for the night?"

"Yes. I would love to go to sleep now."

I gave Mom her sleeping pill and a kiss and said good night.

I walked out of her room and over to the desk to tell the nurse on duty that Mom had been given her sleeping pill and was down for the night. I asked her to call me if there were any problems, no matter what time of the night. She said that she would and told me not to worry; Mom was in good hands.

Chapter 17

The next morning, I drove the kids to school at eight and then went straight to the hospital. I walked into Mom's room to find another patient lying in her bed. I stopped dead in my tracks. In a panic, I ran up to the nurse's desk and asked, "Where's my mom!"

The nurse saw how upset I was and apologized profusely. She pointed down a long hallway and said that Mom had been moved to the room at the end. I noticed that it was quite a distance from the nurse's station.

Relieved, I walked down the hall into a very long and narrow room with one other empty bed. Mom was positioned at the very end of the room, by the window. Her eyes were closed, so as quietly as I could, I walked over to her bed. I noticed a tray of solid food had been placed on the table in front of her. Perturbed, I wondered why they did this. The nurses knew that she could only have liquids.

I didn't like the fact that Mom was being teased by food that she couldn't eat. Annoyed, I moved the tray onto the other bed, sat down on the chair beside Mom, and looked out the window. The day was dark and dreary, and her room seemed to mirror the conditions that were outside.

After a couple of hours, Mom opened her eyes. I got out of my chair, said hello, and gave her a kiss on the cheek. She was very distant.

She asked coldly, "How are you?"

"I'm okay. Are you alright Mom? You seem a little distressed."

With a lot more conviction, she said, "Well, what the hell do you expect? Would you be happy lying around like this, all alone?"

Oh boy, I thought, we have a problem on our hands.

I questioned, "Mom, did something happen to upset you since you've moved here? You were so content last night."

"I'm just fed up with this whole damn thing. I can't do anything anymore. I just lie here. I can't watch television, and I can't read. I can only think for so long, and I'm tired of thinking."

Sympathetically I said, "I wish I could change this for you, Mom. It must be so frustrating, and you must be feeling so angry."

"Well I've been having my moments lately."

"Good, Mom. And so you should. It's about time you got mad because you've been far too nice through all of this. You need to let your anger and frustration out, and I don't mind listening to you at all."

Mom lay quietly and looked out the window. She didn't say much more after that, and I didn't want to pester her into talking. She had these short bouts of anger that never lasted very long. I really didn't know what to say to her to make her feel better; I felt so inadequate. I hated this waiting around for her to die: it was such a helpless feeling.

Mom dozed off again, so I sat quietly reading until just before three o'clock. I got up and whispered in Mom's ear that I had to pick up the kids from school and that I would be back after dinner. She smiled and said that would be fine and dozed off again.

On my way out of the hospital, I told the nurse that Mom couldn't eat solids and I didn't want food to be placed in front of her when she couldn't eat any of it.

The nurse said, "We just thought that if she wanted to try and eat something, she would have it there."

I said, "It's not that she doesn't want it, it's just that she can't stomach it. She would love to eat, but whatever she eats or even drinks comes right back up. I just don't think it's right that she is reminded about what she's missing."

The nurse said, "You're right. I'll make sure that doesn't happen again."

"Just give her juice, and it would be nice if someone could open it for her," I added with a touch of sarcasm. "As you know, she's too weak to do it herself."

ॐ✍

I returned to the hospital after dinner. I couldn't believe my eyes when I walked in and saw another dinner tray on Mom's table. No one had come in to take the lid off the tray, let alone give her some juice. Mom wasn't capable of holding onto a cup or lifting her head at all anymore, so how in the hell did they expect her to organize a food tray. I was furious. I walked over to Mom's bed and removed the tray.

I found Mom in a very depressed state.

"Mom, you look so sad. What's wrong?"

"I've been lying here for hours, trying to figure out what I'm doing in this place. Am I going to lie here in this lonely room until I die?"

I took a deep breath, and then reluctantly replied, "Yes Mom, you are."

She started to cry and as the tears ran down her cheeks, she said, "How did I end up here? This is a horrible place to die. I'm just going to have to lay here and wait for death. I don't want to die in a hospital alone."

"Mom, you don't have to die here; you can come home to our place. It's not natural to die in an institution. It's more natural to die at home, surrounded by the people you love and who love you."

Mom brightened up a bit. She grabbed my hand and held it tightly. "Oh, Carole, can you handle me? She paused and continued, "What about the kids; this could upset them."

"Mom, death is a natural process. It is not something that we should be afraid of. It will be good for the kids to see that death isn't something you hide away, pretending that it's not happening."

As I was saying these words to Mom, I could feel fear welling up inside of me. Her question 'Could I handle this' was a very good one. I wasn't sure how I would cope, but what else was I to do? I knew I had to try for her sake. It was important that Mom had a peaceful death, and I knew that wasn't going to happen if she stayed in the hospital. I resolved I would give every bit of my energy to make this happen. I just prayed that I could pull it off.

Mom dried her eyes and said, "I feel so much better now. I feel as if a weight has been lifted off my chest."

"Good, Mom. I'm glad. Don't worry anymore; you're coming home to your family."

Mom said angrily, "I hate this room. I'm far from the nurse's desk, where they don't have to bother with me."

"What do you mean Mom?"

She said, "After you left last night, they moved me to this room. I felt so angry about being shoved away that I pushed my water glass and vase of flowers off my table with a sweep of my arm. Everything went crashing onto the floor. I could hear the nurses in the hall asking, 'What was that noise?' I could hear them running up and down the hall, checking all the rooms to see where the noise came from, but do you know what, they didn't come and check my room."

With sadness in her voice, she said, "I realized then that I was really alone. I felt really frightened and thought, "What if I had fallen out of bed? There would have been no one to help me."

I patted her hand. "Mom, that's all behind you now. You're coming home with us, so you don't have to think about this anymore. The nurses here are really good, Mom; they're just over-worked. They should have checked on you, for sure, but they probably assumed you were too weak to make that kind of noise."

Mom said, "The nurse came in well over an hour later and cleaned up the mess. No one checked on me before that."

Just then, Corky walked into the room.

Holding Mom's hand he said, "Hi Anne, how are you?"

I didn't give Mom a chance to answer.

I said, "Mom and I were just talking, and she wants to come back home to stay with us. She feels very alone here."

Corky leaned over and gave Mom a kiss on the forehead and said, "The hospital isn't a great place to be. We would love to have you come home with us again."

Mom looked at Corky gratefully, and replied, "Thank you so much. I hope this won't be too much for all of you. I've been so much work lately, and I am truly sorry."

"Don't you worry, Anne. We love you, and you should be at home with us. It will be fine; we'll all get through this together."

151

Mom had a big smile on her face. All signs of depression were gone.

I went out of the room to look for the nurse and found her at the desk. I told her that Mom wanted to come home with us.

She said, "I'm so glad to hear that because, trust me, this is no place to die. I'd rather be put out on the streets than die here."

I was surprised by her frank response. She obviously felt the same way we did.

She continued, "I can get the ambulance to bring your mom home in the morning."

"Okay, but I have a problem. How am I going to help Mom to the bathroom? She can't get up by herself, and I can't lift her."

"We could use a catheter with a urine bag. You will have to empty it regularly into a bucket and then into the toilet."

I went back to Mom and asked her how she felt about having a catheter instead of getting up to go to the bathroom. She said that she didn't mind at all. If that's what it took to go home, it was fine with her.

I said, "They're going to put a catheter in first thing tomorrow. The ambulance will bring you home around ten o'clock in the morning."

Mom's face lit up again and with a big smile she said, "That sounds wonderful! I'm going to be able to have a good sleep tonight just knowing that I will be leaving here soon. I can't wait."

We settled Mom for the night. It was nice to see her somewhat back to her peaceful self. We said good night, and I told her that I would be waiting for her at home in the morning.

࿇

The ambulance arrived just after ten o'clock the next morning. I walked out of the house and into the fall air to greet Mom. They brought Mom out of the ambulance on a stretcher. As they were carrying her to the back door, she said excitedly, "What a lovely day it is! It is so lovely to be outside. She took a deep breath and said,

"Oh, just breathe in this fresh air; the breeze feels so good on my face."

Hearing her say those words made me think of how much I took for granted in my life. I rarely noticed how wonderful the air felt. I was usually in too much of a hurry, rushing here and there; but today I stopped and savored the air on my face too. She was right, it did feel good.

Mom's world had become so refined. She was now in touch with all the subtleties of life and displayed a great reverence for the little things that most of us are too busy to notice.

The ambulance attendants brought Mom into the bedroom and made sure she was comfortable before they left.

Mom was so excited. She reminded me of how a small child acts when something wonderful is happening in their life.

Mom said with great enthusiasm, "I feel great! It's so darn good to be here."

"Well, it's so good to have you here again, too."

The doorbell rang. It was the home care nurse.

I opened the door and immediately remarked, "Wow, Mom's been here for no longer than ten minutes and you're already at our doorstep. I certainly don't mind this fabulous service!"

The nurse chuckled and said in a southern accent, "Yes, we aim to please."

We both laughed, and she said, "I'm so glad your mom is back at your house. The atmosphere here is so much better than the hospital."

"That's for sure; the hospital isn't a great place to be at the best of times. Come in. Mom's in the bedroom."

After the nurse had finished her duties with Mom, she came into the kitchen to talk with me.

She asked, "Are you prepared for Anne dying here in your home? Do you know what to expect when the dying process begins?"

I said, "I really don't have a clue about what's going to happen to Mom. To be honest, I'm kind of scared."

I took a deep breath and continued, "I've never been around a dying person, let alone someone who has died. I've never seen a dead body in my life."

She said, "The dying process is fairly universal. She may spend a number of days sleeping and not being that aware of her environment. You may find you will have to coax answers from her, and at the end stage she may go into a coma. This may last for one to five days before she dies. Hopefully her pain level won't increase."

I said, "So far the analgesic patches have kept her pain free."

She continued, "I don't think that will change. But if it does, we will just add more pain medication. Right now, it is a matter of waiting until that time comes." She went on, "We're going to make sure you have all the support you need, and I'll get the nurses to stay as long as they can when they come to visit. There are a number of the nurses who have tended to your mom over this last year and would love to spend more time with her."

I gratefully replied, "Thank you so much. I am deeply appreciative of the wonderful support all the nurses have given us and all the support that you are offering now. I really feel overwhelmed with all of this, but I guess the decision about Mom dying at home has been made. I hope I can see this to the end."

"Don't panic; we'll get you lots of help. I'll phone the homemaker service and get someone to come to your place daily. Hospice care will send a volunteer who will come here as often as you need. This will give you lots of breaks."

"Thank you, I think I am going to need a lot of breaks."

The nurse stood up and said she had to leave to tend to her next patient. Shortly after her departure, Dr. Morgan arrived to visit Mom. After some time, he came out of her room and asked if he could talk with me.

He sat down at the kitchen table. "Your mom is in good spirits and seems happy to be here," he said.

"Yes, she seems to be very content. I think she's relieved to be out of the hospital."

"Yes, I think she's very relieved." He paused and then continued, "Carole, there is something I want to tell you about your mom. I think if Anne had stayed in the hospital much longer, she would have died before the weekend. Now that she's back here with her loved ones, it is hard to say when she could die. Realistically speaking, there isn't a lot of time left, maybe a week."

"Yes, I figured that there wouldn't be much more than a week left. I guess it's going to be a day-to-day thing."

"Death is a mystery, and we can rarely calculate the exact time a person passes over." He stood up to leave and said, "I want you to call me if you need anything at all. I'll do my best to help you as much as I can."

As we walked toward the door, I said, "Thank you so much Dr. Morgan for all your support. Mom was right about you, and I am so glad you are her doctor."

"And I'm glad I am your Mom's doctor." He smiled and then said, "I'll be back to visit in a few days time."

I walked into Mom's room. She was looking out the window at the stunning view. The fall leaves on the trees were turning a bright, vivid, fluorescent yellow. They were so bright that it was almost too difficult to look at them.

As I was sitting down on the chair beside her, she turned to me, and reaching for my hand, she said, "Thank you for bringing me home, I feel so safe and peaceful here with you."

"I'm so glad you are here with us, Mom. I would be so worried if you were at the hospital. This just seems so right, you being here."

She squeezed my hand and smiled sleepily. "I've had a busy morning. I think I'm going to have a nap for a while," she said.

"I'm glad you feel peaceful, Mom. I'll be out in the kitchen. Call me if you need anything." I leaned over, gave her a kiss and added, "It's so nice to have you back home with us."

࿐

Later that afternoon, the kids arrived home from school. Before I could stop them, they ran into Grandma's bedroom and jumped on her bed with boundless enthusiasm. They began talking about their busy day at school.

155

As I stood in the doorway watching the three of them talking and laughing, I knew at that moment that I had made the right decision to have Mom at our home to die. It was the right thing to do. She was laughing and smiling at their stories, and, for the moment, she appeared very happy.

After dinner, Nigel went into Mom's room with a book and asked her if she would like him to read to her.

Nigel was in a Grade Two French Immersion program. He began to read to Mom in French for a good ten minutes. I stood at the door, watching the two of them together. It was priceless to see. At one point, Mom looked up, smiled at me, and shook her head in amusement.

I thought what a wonderful picture this was. If only I could capture this moment forever. For years it had been Grandma reading to Nigel, and now that Mom couldn't read anymore, Nigel was proudly reading to Grandma.

I had to interrupt them, "Sorry to stop you Nigel, but Grandma's nurse is here."

"Okay. Grandma, I'll read some more to you tomorrow."

"Okay. I'm looking forward to it. I really enjoyed your reading."

Nigel leaned over and gave her a kiss, then crawled off the bed and said, "I'm going to read to you every day Grandma, but right now I'm going to watch TV. I'll come and say goodnight when you're ready."

Mom had a big grin from ear to ear and said, "That would be nice Nigel," as he ran out of the room.

"Don't worry, Mom. I'll try not to put you through that too many times."

Mom and I both chuckled.

After the nurse had settled Mom for the night, the kids, Corky, and I went in to Mom's room and wished her a goodnight. Just before I turned out the light, Mom said, "I'm so happy to be here. I feel safe and sound."

"We're so glad you're here too, Mom. We love you so much. Sleep tight."

Chapter 18

It was Halloween, and the kids were busy putting their costumes on for the big event. Tess was a French maid, Nigel was Frankenstein, and his best friend Carson arrived at our house dressed up as a devil.

Before roaming the neighborhood, they went into Mom's room to show off their costumes. The three of them had a great time entertaining Mom and making her laugh. After a lot of hullabaloo, I ushered them out of the room saying that it was time to start their trick-or-treating. They raced out the door in a whirl, with Nigel yelling excitedly, "Bye Grandma, I'll give you some candy when I get back!"

Corky had offered to stay at the house and give out candy while I went trick-or-treating around the neighborhood with the kids.

I was thankful that Tess and Nigel could continue on with their lives despite what was happening to their Grandma. They didn't seem any the worse for the wear, even with all the trials that our family was going through. Children were so resilient, and I saw how much I could learn from them.

Finally after two hours of knocking on doors, we arrived home around eight o'clock with a big stash of candy.

Corky said that the nurse had been and gone, and Mom was asleep for the night. The kids dumped their bags of goodies on the living room carpet, counted their loot, and then went off to bed with me trailing right behind them.

かや

The next morning after the kids had left for school, I went into Mom's room, apple juice in hand, to wake her up. I opened the blinds and then helped her into a sitting position.

Unfortunately, Mom had developed bed sores over the last month, and her skin had become tender with the lack of movement. There didn't seem to be any position that was comfortable for her anymore. We had tried many things to make the bed softer, and the only thing that helped the most was a lamb's wool blanket.

I poured myself a cup of coffee, pulled up a chair beside Mom's bed, and we began to chat.

She said, "I had a dream last night about my brothers, Charlie and John. I dreamt a most incredible dream. I was walking down the streets of Glasgow. I was going into many of the stores I used to shop at when I was a young girl. Many of the shopkeepers were in the dream, and I even remembered their names. I had completely forgotten about all these people. It really was a wonderful dream."

I said, "I can't remember when your brothers died."

"Oh, it's been years, but in my dream Charlie and John looked like they did when they were young. They told me that they were looking forward to seeing me again soon."

In silence, I mulled over what she said. The book *Final Gifts* talked about loved ones from the other side coming to the dying person, and I wondered if this was happening to Mom.

"Mom, do you think they're coming to get you?"

"I don't know, but the dream was so real."

We sat quietly for a few moments. There was a definite change in her. She seemed dreamier, as if she wasn't completely present. Her speech was slower and her sentences were shorter; they were not so elaborate. Mom's ability to concentrate had waned, and she wasn't interested in talking as much as she had before. I knew that a new stage had begun.

૭≪

Even though there were many peaceful times for Mom, there were still moments where she became very agitated. I intuitively knew that she still had things that were unfinished in her life. I didn't know what they were, and perhaps she didn't either. I realized that I had to help her clarify and clear up as many of these loose ends as I could.

One of the loose ends I thought about was whether or not she would like to speak with a minister. I decided to question her about this.

I asked, "Would you like to have someone who can give you spiritual guidance come to the house?

She said, "Actually, I have been thinking about that, and yes, I would very much like to see a minister." She paused for a moment, "We attended the United Church years ago, so maybe there is someone there who I could talk to."

Mom had her own personal connection with God but hadn't had any interest in going to church for most of her life. But facing her death now, she began questioning whether there was anything beyond this life. Maybe a minister would be able to help her get through this very difficult time.

I told her that I would phone the church right away. She was pleased with this decision and then said that she would like to rest for awhile. I left her dozing.

I left the room to phone the United Church and was lucky to talk to a minister named Brian Jones. I explained about my Mother's illness and how she would like to speak to him when he had time. Luckily, he had a few hours free that same afternoon and would come over after lunch. I was surprised at how quickly he responded to our need.

I felt a little uneasy as I hung up. I hadn't been a church-going person, and I wasn't sure what I should say to him. I worried that he might talk to Mom about hell and damnation which would undoubtedly upset her.

These thoughts brought back memories of an encounter I had had years ago with a group of born-again Christians. This group of four women had severely judged me because I leaned toward Eastern philosophies, which didn't coincide with their interpretation of God. They had told me I was going straight to hell if I didn't become a Christian. This had been one of the most disturbing encounters in my life. I hoped that he wasn't that kind of minister.

Reverend Jones knocked on the door at twelve thirty. I opened the door to a very tall man with snow white hair and a twinkle in his beautiful, soft blue eyes. Smiling, he humbly put out his hand to shake mine and then said in a soft Irish accent, "Hello Carole, I'm Reverend Jones. It's nice to meet you."

Many of my reservations began to fall away; I instantly liked him. I could see that he was a kind and compassionate man.

"I'm so glad you could come to our home Reverend Jones. My mother is thrilled that you could find the time to visit with her."

I guided him to Mom's room and introduced Reverend Jones to her.

Mom smiled and said, "Please, come in and have a seat."

He walked over to her bedside chair and sat down. He reached for her hand and, holding it, he asked how she was doing. Mom looked almost shy, maybe even a bit embarrassed, at meeting someone new in such an informal way. She seemed so vulnerable with him. I could see that this was what she needed. It was important for her to talk to someone who was devoted to God and who was able to fill a void that no one else could. I think she needed assurance that she was going to be alright and to have him to pray with her and for her. I left them alone. A half hour later, Reverend Jones asked me to come back into the room.

He softly began, "Your mother has asked me to preside at her funeral."

I was so relieved that he had brought up the issue of her funeral. It had crossed my mind many times over the last month, but I just didn't know how to approach the subject with Mom.

He continued, "Your mom would like the funeral at the United Church. She's requested to be cremated and would like her ashes to be buried in the rose garden beside the church."

That was a big issue resolved; one more piece of unfinished business was now finished. Now Mom could hopefully get on with the process of dying in peace.

Reverend Jones could see that Mom was getting tired and needed to rest; he patted her on the hand and said that he would be back to visit soon.

We left Mom and walked into the kitchen. Out of courtesy,

I asked Reverend Jones if he would like a cup of tea, and, to my surprise, he accepted. We went into the living room and sat on the couch with our cookies and tea.

Reverend Jones said with concern, "Helping a loved one journey to the other side can be much harder for the caretaker than the person who is dying. I hope you are taking care of yourself in all of this."

I said, "Yes, but it's been exhausting. I think the hardest thing in all of this is how much I am going to miss her. But saying that, I do know she is going to be fine. Death is a natural part of life. I guess I see death as a transition to a different state of consciousness for Mom; she will be free of her tired, sick body."

To my surprise, he agreed.

I went on, "I am not traditional in my spiritual beliefs, and I would say that I lean more toward Eastern philosophy."

I explained that I had lived in India for a year and that I found Buddhists to be one of the most peaceful and loving people I had ever met.

He said, "I lived in India for five years, and I found the people to be exceptional also. God comes through each of us in a different way; it's really about what's in your heart that counts."

I knew then that this man was very special. He was not a Christian man who was judgmental and rigid in his faith. He had seen enough to be open minded and accepting of other people's beliefs. I was relieved and found myself becoming more comfortable with each passing moment.

I said, "I wouldn't call Mom a religious person. She always believed that there was something greater but never really put a name to it. She would often say, 'I think there must be a God as there does seem to be some sort of plan for us all.'"

Sheepishly, I said, "To be honest, I'm surprised that she wanted to see a minister."

He smiled and said, "Many people, on their death bed, want and need assurance that they're going to be all right after they die. It is a scary time for everyone. Letting go of all that you are, and all that you have known, is very difficult."

He paused, "Many people have deep regrets and wish that they had done some things in their life differently. The dying person needs to know that everything is going to be alright and that God loves them no matter what. A reverend can help put their guilt and pain behind them and then they can die in peace."

I added, "I think this is exactly what's happening to Mom. She seems to be hanging on longer than we ever expected. I hope she can let go and move on now that she has spoken to you about the afterlife."

"I am so glad that you brought up her funeral. That must have been a big relief for Mom to talk about what she wanted. I didn't know how to broach that subject, and now that has been cleared up, she can put all that to rest."

He said, "Carole, this is a difficult time. If you need anything at all, please call me. I will help you and your mother as much as I can. I have to go now as I have another appointment, but I'll keep in touch with you on a daily basis."

I thanked him very much, and we said goodbye. I knew we were lucky to have someone like him come into our lives at this time. It didn't matter that our beliefs were somewhat different from one another; there was still a common bond and a respect between us. I was very thankful for that.

I looked in on Mom and asked her if she had enjoyed talking to Reverend Jones.

She said, "I really like him. He is such a kind man. He told me that it didn't matter that I didn't go to church. It's what's in our hearts that counts."

"I think that is so true, and I'm glad you like him Mom. I think he is a wonderful man."

Mom yawned and said, "I'm tired. I'd like to go to sleep for awhile."

"It's been an emotional day for you, and a nap will be good. I have to get the kids. Are you going to be alright for ten minutes?"

"Oh sure, I'll just be dozing. Go ahead."

I arrived home just in time to meet Mom's nurse at the door. She tended to Mom and then came and spoke with me.

She said, "Your mom is so dreamy and quiet. She seems a lot more distant now."

"Yes, I've noticed that too. She has a lot more clarity first thing in the morning, but even then she's still a little distant. She's losing contact with us; it's becoming obvious that she is detaching from the world."

After the nurse left, I walked to the bedroom, stopped in the doorway, and observed Mom. She looked so content and peaceful. She was sitting with her hands folded in her lap, gazing off into the far distance. I wasn't sure how to approach her in times like these. There was a distinct change in her consciousness: ever so subtle, but it was there. She was off somewhere else a lot more often than not these days. I quietly turned and walked out of the room; I didn't want to interrupt her space.

Mom was in a dream state for most of the day. Close to her bedtime she said, "What a wonderful day I had today. I feel so peaceful and happy."

I said, "I noticed that you seemed to be somewhere else for most of the day. You're quite dreamy these days, you know."

"I feel dreamy and peaceful. It was a wonderful day."

I smiled and pulled the covers up to her chin.

"I love you Mom. Have a good sleep, and remember: Ring your bell if you need anything at all."

"I'll ring if I need to. I love you too, sweetheart. Goodnight."

I knew she wouldn't ring the bell. She never did. She didn't want to wake me, and so far I hadn't had to get up once in the night to tend to her. She seemed to manage the nights quite well thanks to the patches.

I had heard many stories that pain control was one of the most difficult problems for people dying of cancer. Mom would have been in a lot of pain if it wasn't for these patches that consistently kept her pain free. I was so thankful for that.

Chapter 19

The morning arrived much sooner than I expected. I found it difficult to wake up from the deep sleep I was in. The pressure of being a caregiver was taking its toll on me; I was emotionally and physically exhausted. I wondered how much longer I could handle this stress.

I opened my eyes and forced myself out of bed to get the kids ready for school. I thought about how the kids' busy lives continued on as usual; they appeared impervious to what was happening. Mom was still with us, so in their minds she was safe and sound. Everything was okay.

The kids gobbled up their breakfast, left a mess, and got into to the van with Corky. I waved goodbye as they drove out of the driveway. I closed the door and turned to the chaos staring at me in the kitchen. I thought, here I am stuck in the house again, cleaning up after everyone. I turned and walked out of the kitchen, deciding that I was going to avoid the disarray for as long as possible. I went into Mom's room and found her wide awake.

I opened up the blind on her window to another beautiful fall day.

"Hi Mom, how are you feeling today?"

She complained, "My hips are aching a bit, but other than that I feel good."

"Here Mom, let's turn you over."

I put my arm around her shoulder and hip. As I turned her, I noticed that she was the size of a ten year old girl, so tiny and lightweight. Her hip was exposed, and as I pulled down her nightgown, I could see her hip bone accentuated by sagging skin. I wondered how a human being could possibly continue to survive in this state.

Mom sighed, "Ahhh that feels so much better. Could I have something to drink?"

I brought Mom a glass of juice. She took a few small sips, smacked her lips with pleasure and said, "Boy that tastes good!"

With a cup of coffee in hand, I sat down to have a chat with her.

Mom said, "A wonderful thing happened last night. Leif came to visit me and said that he's finally coming to take me home soon."

Looking at her in silence, I could feel a lump form in my throat as so many thoughts swirled around in my head. The end for Mom was coming soon; I knew that. I thought I would feel relief, but instead I felt absolute panic at the notion of her dying.

With difficulty, I summoned up an excited tone in my voice. "Mom, that's incredible! What did Leif say to you?"

Mom had a warm smile on her face as she proclaimed happily, "Leif loves me very much, and he is so happy that we will be together again. He says that when I go over to the other side, we will talk about what happened at his death and we'll talk about all the years that we have been apart. We're going to catch up."

"What do you mean the other side?"

"It's where everyone goes when they die. This isn't home, you know. We are only visitors here on earth. Our true home is on the other side. It's where we are our real selves—who we really are. We are not this physical body at all. I understand that now."

"I see. So what is the other side like?" I asked.

Unexpectedly, she closed her eyes and went into a trance-like state. I called her name a few times, but she wouldn't answer me.

I waited for a few moments, and then she opened her eyes and said, "I'd like another drink and then I'd like to rest."

I decided not to pressure her with any more questions. I would talk to her about this a little later.

She took a few sips of juice and closed her eyes.

"Okay Mom, I need to clean the kitchen anyway. The nurse should be here soon. Call if you need me."

I looked in on Mom a while later. She was sitting quietly, staring at the wall. It was as if she wasn't seeing it, but was seeing through it with a glassy-eyed stare. She was so peaceful, with a slight smile on her face; it appeared as if she was concentrating and listening to something or someone. I wondered what she was experiencing.

She didn't notice me standing in the room. I watched her for the longest time, yet she never became aware of my presence. Finally, I turned and quietly left the room. She was certainly changing; she was leaving us. I could see that.

Later that morning, the nurse and the homemaker arrived at my doorstep almost at the same time. It was always such a relief to see these women.

The homemaker was a tiny woman in her thirties named Eva. She was very sensitive to our situation and always did more work than her job description required. Eva was very gentle with Mom and was aware of how vulnerable and frail she was. I felt confident in leaving Mom in her care. I told Eva that I had a few errands to do around town, and that I would be back shortly.

ॐ॰ॐ

I arrived home a few hours later to find Mom bathed and sitting up in a freshly changed bed.

She smiled at me and said, "You're back. Did you get everything done?

"Yes, pretty much. Are you up for a visit Mom?"

"Sure, I feel pretty good right now."

I sat down and held her hand. "Cheerfully," I asked, "So, Mom, how are you feeling this afternoon?"

She looked at me with a lovely smile on her face and said, "I have been visiting with the angels. They used to come and go, but now they are going to stay with me until I leave."

I was taken aback. I collected myself and asked, "What angels? You have never mentioned angels before. It sounds like they have been here a few times."

"Yes, they have been coming and going. But these ones are different; they are the angels that have come to take me home."

"So there's more than one? How many angels are there?"

"Oh, there are many, many angels."

I didn't know what other questions to ask, so I asked one off the top of my head. It was a ridiculous question to ask, but I asked anyway: "What color are the angels?

"They are every color of the rainbow." She sighed, "They are so beautiful. We sit and talk for hours, and they tell me that I will be going home soon."

Happily she said, "Oh Carole, I just can't wait to go. Where I am going is so incredible and so beautiful. If only you could see it."

I excitedly asked a few questions in a row—What is it like on the other side? Where are you going? What's the place like?—but to no avail; she had closed her eyes.

I called her name, trying to get her to answer me, but her face had gone blank. It was as if she had fallen into a deep sleep. I was perplexed by this behavior. I waited eagerly until she opened her eyes and looked at me again.

With anticipation, I asked once more, "Mom, what is the other side like?"

Again she closed her eyes and wouldn't respond to my question. Now I was getting impatient. I wondered why she was acting this way.

I began gently coaxing her, "Mom can you hear me? She opened her eyes again. I then continued, "Every time I ask you what the other side is like, you blank out and you won't answer my question. Mom, I really need to know."

"I'm sorry Carole, but I am not allowed to tell you what it's like. You have to wait your turn. If you knew how beautiful it is on the other side, you wouldn't want to be here anymore. You would spend all your time yearning to be on the other side instead of fully being here in this physical existence. She then paused and light-heartedly added, "But don't you worry, it won't be long until you're there with me."

I was stunned. How could she say that? I thought, Oh my God! Was I going to die soon? Chills went up my spine. Then it dawned on me that for her, the concept of time had changed. She had already moved to that place where time didn't exist.

I was frustrated. I've always been very curious about life after death, and it really irritated me that she was not going to give me more information than that. She was giving me bits and pieces that whetted my appetite but nothing more.

I tried to ask her more questions but she wouldn't budge. She was very sleepy by this time and wanted to have a nap, so I gave up and let her be.

As the days went by, Mom began responding in much shorter sentences. She was very distracted and became irritated when I tried to get her to elaborate on anything that she said. When she became like that, I just knew to back off and drop the subject.

Chapter 20

The door bell rang early the next morning. It was my friend Cheryl, handing me a plate overflowing with chocolate chip cookies. She was continually bringing us something sweet and delicious to eat since Mom's arrival at our house.

I thanked her and said, "So here you are again with more goodies. Are you trying to fatten me up?"

She joked, "It certainly wouldn't hurt you. You are rather skinny these days. She smiled and said, "I thought I'd drop by quickly and see if you needed anything."

"That's very nice of you, and now that you've asked, I will take you up on your offer. Could you come to Mom's house with me tomorrow morning? The homemaker will be here, so it will give me time to pick up Mom's mail and check on her house. I could go by myself, but I hate the thought of going into her house alone."

I paused, "I don't know why, but the last time I went by myself, I felt nervous, almost scared: as if someone was in the house and they were going to jump out at me. Maybe it's because it feels so unlived in."

"Carole, I would feel the same way. For sure I will come with you. I have most of the day free, so why don't I pick you up at around ten o'clock?"

"That's fine. I really appreciate this, Cheryl. Thanks so much."

She said, "I am off to the dentist. See you tomorrow."

తో ⅍

Vern and Sandy phoned Mom on a daily basis, but with each passing day, Mom was less interested in talking and was always eager to give the phone back to me.

During one of those phone calls, Vern said to me, "Mom sure doesn't say much anymore, and when she does talk her voice is so wispy. I don't think she is that interested in talking with me anymore."

"Don't take it personally; she's losing contact with all of us. I think you should come and visit Mom one more time. She's been saying there are angels around her and that Leif is coming to take her home soon."

I paused and said, "I don't think there is going to be much time left, Vern."

"I think you are right. We had better get there as soon as possible. I'll phone you and let you know when we're coming."

He changed the subject and asked, "How are you handling all of this? Are you doing alright?"

"Oh, I'm okay I guess—just emotionally tired. Luckily, she never wakes me up in the night, so I get a pretty good sleep which helps me cope in the day time. She tries not to disturb me, and she's not demanding at all. It's more the strain of having to watch her die that is so hard."

Vern said, "You're giving Mom a wonderful gift, Carole. You won't regret doing this for her."

I said, "Well it's been the hardest thing I've ever undertaken, but I'm glad I decided to have Mom here with us to die. At least I'll know in the end that I did everything I could for her with little regret. I just wish the outcome could be different."

"I know. I wish it could be different too, but there's only one way this is going to end," said Vern.

"Yes, and there is no easy way out of this," I acknowledged. "Well, Vern, nice talking with you, but I have to get going. I'll talk to you tomorrow."

∂∞◌

The next morning, I found Mom looking very depressed. I had never seen her mouth turned down as low as it was on this day. She was despondent and would hardly reply to any of my questions.

Concerned, I asked, "Mom, what's wrong? You're very sad."

With a touch of anger in her voice she said, "They won't come and get me. They won't come and take me home. They stand around looking at me and talking to me, but they won't take me."

I tried to think of something to say that would appease her, to give her answers as to why this was happening.

"Mom, remember, they told you they are going to take you home, but maybe it's not time yet."

Adamantly she said, "I don't care. I can't stand this any longer. Why is this happening to me, and why do I have to keep lying here day in and day out, waiting to go? It's so frustrating because I know exactly where I'm going, but I can't get there."

All of a sudden her demeanor changed. In a split second, a startled look came over her face: her eyes widened, and she appeared very afraid. Then, just as quickly, she relaxed and with a big smile she excitedly said, "Oh, it's my mother! My mother is here!"

She was quiet for a moment and then said, "She's here. I can see her and I can feel her holy spirit. She is coming closer. Oh, thank God she is here!"

I put my hand on her arm to pacify her, and once again she was calm. I had never heard my mom use the term 'holy spirit'. This was beyond strange.

I asked, "Mom, why were you so frightened?"

"I seem to get caught between two worlds. It's been happening a lot lately. I don't seem to belong to either place, here or there. I get caught somewhere in the middle, and I don't know where I am. When I'm in that space, I feel very lost and it scares me. But this time, my mother came to help me and I felt protected."

"Is your mother with you now?"

"Oh yes, she is. She is so beautiful, just like she was when I was a child. She will stay with me now until I leave."

"Why don't you ask her why you haven't gone home yet?"

"I just did, and she said that I can come home whenever I want to."

I was confused by this statement. On the one hand, she could go whenever she wanted; but on the other hand, she wasn't leaving. This was very perplexing, and as I pondered what she had just said, the light bulb went on: something was still holding her here—something that she hadn't finished.

I said, "Mom, are you still hanging on because of me? Are you worried about me?"

"Yes, I am worried that you won't be okay."

I knew I had to reassure her, so I said with conviction, "Mom I'll be okay. I will miss you so much, but I will be just fine."

As I said these words, I realized that I wasn't so sure that I would be fine. I knew I wasn't telling her the truth because the real truth was that I didn't know if I would be okay. That's when I saw that it was me. I was the problem. I was hanging on to her; it wasn't the other way around. I was keeping her alive because of *my* need for her.

I knew then that I had to convince her that I would be fine. I had told her many times in the past that it was alright for her to die, but she knew that I didn't really mean it.

I assured her again, "Mom, it's okay to go to the other side. I know you will be with me."

"Carole, I will always be with you. You can count on that."

"Then go, Mom. Let go and be with your mom and Leif."

She didn't answer me. She just closed her eyes and appeared to drift off into her own world. I was learning that this was her signal that she had talked enough. I quietly walked to the door, and I left her room.

If anyone had listened to our conversations over those last few days, they probably would have questioned Mom's mental health and maybe even mine. But I knew that she was very much in control of all her mental faculties. Her clarity hadn't changed; she was still as bright as she had always been. What had changed was the depth of her communication; she had acquired unfathomable wisdom that I had never heard her express at any time in the past. There was no doubt that she was a lot closer to the afterlife than I had ever been, so who was I to question what she had been telling me?

I'd often wondered if angels were real or just imaginary. Many religions spoke about them and gave the impression that they existed; but I had doubts about their existence, and Mom definitely hadn't believed in angels up to a week ago. I pondered this thought, and I had to admit I found it an appealing concept to think that angels were around us. It was very comforting for me to think that Mom was under their wings while she transitioned over to the other side.

∂∞∾

Later that evening, Corky arrived home from work just in time to sit down to dinner. As we were eating, I told him about the conversation I'd had that afternoon with Mom and what she was experiencing.

With skepticism he said, "Those drugs are probably making her hallucinate."

"That would be an easy explanation, I guess, but the dose hasn't changed in over six weeks, and up until recently, she has been her usual self. It's only been the last week that she's been talking this way."

I continued, "You and I know that Mom is a very rational and pragmatic person. She's the last person I'd expect to be talking about angels and the Holy Spirit coming to her unless it was really happening."

"Well, acknowledged Corky, "you do make some good points, but honestly, I've never experienced any of this stuff before. My mom died of a stroke, and your dad went into diabetic shock. It all happened so fast. This is a very different situation with your mom, and to tell you the truth, I don't know what to think."

"I know," I said. "Being around Mom is showing me how little I know about death. In our society, talking about death is taboo and we avoid talking about it like the plague. We know it's inevitable, and yet it is always a shock when we are faced with our own or our loved one's death, no matter what the age. It seems we are never ready for it."

Corky agreed, "Yah, we're often shocked when we hear about someone dying, even a very old person. Maybe it's our fear of the unknown and our attachments to this physical world. Dying is a tough process, for sure. But the truth is none of us are getting out of here alive; so why don't we learn more about it before we die, and face the inevitable before it happens?

"I know that sounds crazy," he acknowledged, "but I think if we understood death, then, in a way, we would understand living. I think we would all live differently if we really faced our mortality. I believe we wouldn't be so afraid of it and maybe we'd live our lives in a more fulfilling way."

"Yah, that's so true," I agreed. "Most of us don't have a clue how to help a person pass over to the other side. The book I read helped me so much. The author said that it's important to ask the dying person questions about what they're experiencing, give them lots of encouragement to talk about their feelings, and acknowledge what they are saying. The more they are accepted, the more they will open up and share their deepest feelings. I found it interesting that the author mentioned that a dying person will give little tidbits but will not elaborate about what they are experiencing unless they are asked.

"After all," I continued, "what better way to understand death, than from the dying? We just need to spend time with them and really listen to what they are saying."

As I was pondering this last thought, Tess broke the moment by saying, "Dad, it's time for me to go to my ballet class. Are you going to drive me?"

Corky got up from the table and said, "Okay, get your stuff and let's go."

৵৽৻

The nurse arrived at the house shortly after dinner. We went into the room together to help Mom get ready for the night. We noticed that there was very little urine in her bag, and the little that was there was very thick and sludge-like. The nurse said that jelly-like urine was one of the signs that the kidneys were shutting down; death was very close. The nurse felt there were only a few days left.

After Mom was settled, I walked the nurse to the door, said goodbye then went back into Mom's room. She seemed barely conscious of my presence, and she just whispered "night" ever so softly. I closed the door and wondered if I would be able to talk to her at all the next day. Would she be in a coma? Would she still be alive?

Mom's face was very gaunt, with her cheekbones and eyes being the prominent facial features. I could not imagine living as long as she had in this condition. She had suffered so much.

I hated this horrible waiting game that we were all playing. I felt guilty; a part of me just wanted Mom to die so that she was out of her misery and I could get on with living. My life had stopped a year ago, and I was in this bizarre nightmare that would not end until she died. It was hard to imagine leading a normal life again. I was so caught up in my mom's life—first her illness, and now her death—but there hadn't been any choice. I had taken on this responsibility, and now I had to follow through and make Mom's last days as comfortable and peaceful as possible. But how much longer could I go on? I was exhausted and I wasn't sure if I could handle much more. Even simple tasks like going to the grocery store and paying bills seemed to be too much for me these days.

I was beginning to feel disconnected from everything, and I definitely needed a break. But how do you take a break when you are orchestrating someone's death? There is no time off until it is over. I was on automatic pilot, tuned into one channel.

I leaned on the kitchen wall, closed my eyes, and began fantasizing that when all this was over, I would go to a nice tropical island somewhere, lie on the beach, and soak up the sun for at least two weeks. I could see myself lying on the hot, white sand in my bathing suit. I was so engrossed in these thoughts that I could almost smell the ocean and feel the sun on my skin. I opened my eyes, gave myself a shake back into reality, then walked to the sink and began washing the pots that were waiting for me.

I finished cleaning up as quickly as I could and crawled straight into bed. It was only eight thirty, but I needed to get to sleep. I didn't want to think about another thing. As I drifted off, I could not help but wish that when I woke up in the morning I would be somewhere else, and none of this was really happening to me.

≈◈

I awoke early the next morning, feeling apprehensive about the day ahead of me. Would Mom still be alive when I went to check on her? If so, would she be alert or would she be off somewhere else and not be able to communicate with me anymore? I got out of bed and put my housecoat on. I went down the stairs and stood in front of her door; I dreaded walking in. I knew I had no choice, so I took a deep breath and opened her bedroom door.

To my surprise, Mom was awake. She turned her head and looked at me and said, "Hi, how are you?"

Relieved, I said, "I'm fine, Mom. Did you sleep okay?"

"Hmm, pretty good. Can you help me sit up please?"

I moved Mom to a more comfortable position and gave her a drink of juice. I was thrilled to find she was her usual self again. Her speech was slow and soft, but she wanted to communicate.

I started our conversation by saying, "I'm going over to your place today, Mom. The last time I was at your house, I noticed that you have a few colostomy bags and flanges in the bathroom, so I will bring them here. I also need to pick up your mail. You probably have a few bills that I'm going to have to pay. You know, telephone, heat, and electricity."

Mom said, "Yes, and it would be a good idea to make sure the house is securely locked up."

She hesitated, "I've been meaning to ask you Carole, do you think I should get Christmas presents for the kids? I've been thinking about this, and I don't know if that would upset them on Christmas morning to have presents from me when I'm not there."

Looking at Mom, I thought about her question. I didn't know what to say at first. Mom had a good point about them being upset.

After a moment, I said, "Mom, Christmas presents aren't important right now. I wouldn't worry about them."

Mom decided, "I think it would upset them at Christmas."

"I think you're right, Mom."

Mom looked down at her hands as we pondered the same thing. This would be the first Christmas we wouldn't be together.

The door bell rang and broke the moment.

I said, "That must be the homemaker. I am going to go to your house while she's here. I won't be long, Mom."

Cheryl arrived shortly after the homemaker to drive me to Mom's house. It wasn't easy going inside; it made me sad knowing that she wouldn't be coming back to her home ever again.

As I was packing Mom's personal items, Cheryl came in from outside and said, "Carole, come and see your mom's beautiful garden. The flowers are so gorgeous. Let's pick a bouquet for her."

I walked outside to Mom's garden; the flowers were indeed very beautiful. It was the beginning of November, and I was surprised at how many flowers were still blooming in her garden at this time of the year.

"What a good idea, Cheryl. Since Mom can't come here, we can bring something of her place back to her."

I said, "Mom is going to love these flowers we picked. She's had many flowering plants given to her in the last few months, but these will be special."

We arrived home around noon. We put the flowers in a crystal vase and took them into Mom's room to show her the bouquet. Mom grinned from ear to ear and said, "Oh, what beautiful flowers! Where did you get them?"

"We picked them from your garden."

Mom said, "Oh my, they are so lovely!"

Cheryl put the flowers on the table where Mom could see them. She gave Mom a big hug and said she had to be on her way.

Mom was sleepy; I left her so she could have a nap. I made myself a nice, hot cup of tea and curled up on the couch in the living room. Gazing out the window, it occurred to me how such a simple thing as picking flowers and giving them to someone you love could feel so good. It had given Mom so much joy to have a bouquet of flowers from her garden—flowers that she had tended. I wondered why I hadn't thought of it before now.

ॐॐ

Just as I was clearing the dinner table, Jeannie the home care nurse arrived at our door. She was a plump, jolly person who oozed a lot of warmth and a whole lot of personality. She had to be one of the most nurturing people I had ever met.

Jeannie boldly walked into the house and immediately went into Mom's room, gave her a big hug, and told her how great she looked. After fussing with Mom, because she always fussed with her, she came out of the bedroom and asked me how I was handling everything.

I said, "I'm holding up, I guess. But to be honest, this seems to be going on a long time. I don't know how much longer I can do this. I can hardly remember the last time Corky and I talked about anything other than Mom, her illness, and what we should do with her next. We rarely go anywhere together anymore. Corky has been so patient and understanding. If it were the other way around, I'm not so sure I'd be as supportive. I'd probably be very irritated and frustrated."

Jeannie said, "You're very lucky that he's so accepting of this situation and that he's not adding any more stress than you already have. You guys are doing a great job, and in the end, you'll be glad that you did this for your mom."

She gave me a great big bear hug and said, "You're going to get through this Carole. Call me anytime you need help."

Jeannie always had a way of making me feel that everything was going to be just fine. She inspired me to keep going.

I went into Mom's room to say good night and to remind her that Vern would be here tomorrow. Her eyes were closed. I wasn't sure she was asleep, so I tiptoed over to her and whispered, "Vern will be here tomorrow afternoon." There was no answer, so I asked, "Do you need anything before you go to sleep?"

Mom opened her eyes and dreamily said, "Carole, they're coming to take me home on Sunday."

I was taken aback. That was the day after tomorrow. That wasn't very far away. I said, "Mom that's in two days time. Are you sure?"

"Yes, they told me I'm finally going home."

"Wow, this is a bit of a surprise. That's not very far away; that seems so soon. Are you sure?"

"Carole, you're going to be fine and so are Tess and Nigel. They are going to grow up to be wonderful adults."

What a strange thing to say about the kids, I thought. It's like she was seeing into the future.

With an expression of contentment and tranquility, she added blissfully, "I am finally at peace, and I am really going home this time."

"I'm so glad, Mom; it's taken a long time to come to this place. You must be very happy to finally be going home."

"I am, and I can't wait."

Mom was ready to go to sleep. I gave her a hug, reminded her to ring the bell if she needed me, and said good night.

Chapter 21

MY BROTHER ARRIVED the next afternoon. It was always a relief to see him; the weight instantly melted off my shoulders. He gave me a big hug and then asked to see Mom. I warned him that she had changed since he had seen her last and not to be too alarmed. As Vern walked into Mom's room, his face filled with sadness and empathy; he was having a hard time seeing Mom in this deteriorated state. She had changed dramatically since the last time he was with her.

She softly said, "Hi Vern," but other than his name, she really didn't have much to say. Vern held her hand in silence. He looked heartbroken and a little hurt. She had really distanced herself from all of us, and he could really feel it. I quietly left the room and gave Vern and Mom time to be alone.

After an hour or so, he came out of the bedroom and said, "Mom hardly said a word to me. She doesn't seem to care that I'm visiting her." He looked so dejected.

I gave him a hug saying, "Vern, Mom was really excited about you coming to see her; it has nothing to do with her love for you. One of the reasons she's so distant is because this isn't a good time of day for her. It's best to visit first thing in the morning as she seems more alert then. But saying that, I know what you are saying is true. It's as if she isn't really here anymore; she is moving further and further away from us."

Vern said, "I can't believe how much she has changed in such a short period of time. She's so different."

I put my arm around Vern's waist and said, "I know. We're losing her, but you're here now and she knows that. I think you would have regretted not seeing her one more time, especially since she told me that she's leaving the day after tomorrow."

Vern took a deep breath and said, "Carole, she doesn't seem very lucid anymore. She's probably just confused and doesn't know what she is saying."

"I don't think she's confused at all. She understands much more than we think she does, and we need to give her more credit for that. We need to pay attention to what she is saying and read between the lines. Spending time with Mom has taught me a lot about the dying process. There are so many layers that she needed to dissolve; there is so much that she has to detach from. She is giving us valuable information about death, if we want to listen."

I went on, "Since Mom's illness, I have witnessed her passage of letting go of everything that has had any meaning to her, including her family, and now she's finally come to that place of acceptance that life is over on this physical plane. I'm beginning to understand what happens when a person's life is coming to an end, and how, once everything is resolved, they are so willing and content to move on to the other side. As difficult as the steps can be, it really is an incredible, wonderful journey."

I explained, "Mom has now disengaged from this world and has come to a place of peace. She knows that Leif and her Mom and brothers are waiting to take her home, and with that knowing, there is very little agitation in her anymore. She is so calm and tranquil, but at the same time there is an air of excitement about her. It's as if she knows she is going on a big, wonderful trip and she can't wait to go."

Vern laughed nervously and said, "I don't know; it is way beyond me."

He went back into the bedroom and tried talking to Mom, but she was completely unresponsive this time. Watching Vern doing his best to communicate showed me how in tune I had become with her. I knew what she wanted without her having to say much. Even though her sentences were short, they were very meaningful. Sadly, Vern wasn't in sync. He hadn't been able to spend as much time with her as I had. I felt bad for him; he was walking into something that was so hard to understand.

After dinner, Vern decided to go to Mom's house to sleep for the night. I invited him to stay with us, but he preferred to be on his own. I told him to phone anytime and that we would see him first thing in the morning.

❧

It was early Saturday morning, and I didn't want to get out of bed. I would have loved to have slept longer but I had to get up. I knew Mom's bones would be aching and she would need to roll over. I got up and walked into her room to find her wide awake. I had often wondered what time she awoke and whether she lay quietly for hours, waiting patiently, not wanting to wake me.

I was acutely aware of her vulnerability and her dependence on me that morning. She had accepted the fact that she was helpless and was resigned to this relationship we had with each other.

"Hi Mom, how are you today?"

Mom didn't look at me. She just stared at the wall and said, "Good."

Her eyes didn't flicker.

"Do you want me to move you?"

She said in a pleasant voice, "Yes please."

I had to smile as I thought, she's always so polite. I fluffed Mom's pillows and lifted her into a sitting position. She was so light. I don't think she could have weighed more than eighty pounds.

I gave Mom a sip of juice. I went into the kitchen, poured myself a cup of coffee, and came back to her room and sat beside her. She was very dreamy with a faraway look on her face. It didn't seem that she was up to chatting, and I didn't know what to talk about anyway. I knew that my everyday life with the kids and Corky held very little interest for her anymore; she was too busy dying.

I decided to talk about something from her world, so I asked her if Leif was still with her. She perked up a little and said, "Leif is always here now. He never leaves me anymore."

"What about the angels? Are they still around?"

Mom said in a frank manner, "Of course. They won't leave me until I go to the other side and then the angels will stay here with you."

With excitement in my voice, I said, "They will? Are you sure?"

Mom smiled and said, "Of course they will because whatever I cherish, they will cherish also."

I sat for a moment and pondered what she had just said. I wanted to ask her how long they would stay, but I felt I was asking too much. The lovely thought of angels staying with me was enough for now. The idea that I had angels around me was very reassuring and made me feel very warm inside.

I sat quietly for a few moments, and then I asked, "Do you want me to phone Vern so you can talk with him?"

"Sure."

I dialed Vern's number and held the phone to Mom's ear. She barely spoke a word. I could tell she wasn't interested in talking, so I put the receiver to my ear and asked Vern, "When are you coming over?"

"I was just going out the door when you phoned. I'll see you in a few minutes."

Vern arrived at the house early enough to find Mom somewhat lucid. He spent the morning with her and around lunchtime came out of her room and into the kitchen. He looked at me with such sorrowful eyes and said with deep sadness in his voice, "It's sure hard to talk to her; it's as though my life isn't very important to her anymore. She seems to just want to sleep most of the time."

"I know, but if you ask her questions, she'll usually respond in short answers."

"I noticed that, but she never starts the conversation."

"I think it takes too much energy, Vern; she's very weak. She can't even put her hand around a cup anymore. There's not an ounce of strength left in her."

Vern said, "It's so hard seeing her like this." Shaking his head he said, "I can't believe she is still alive."

I could see that the emotional strain was taking its toll. He was saddened by Mom's distancing compared to the last time when she had been talkative and so happy to see him. He didn't expect her to be so indifferent to his presence. For me, this distancing had been gradual; even though I was aware it was happening, I had slowly been eased into the change. I had learned to not take it personally.

Vern said, "I think I will go back to Mom's house and have an early night. I am really tired."

As I walked Vern to the door, I reminded him, "Mom said she is leaving us tomorrow, and I believe her. I don't know what time, so try and be here early in the morning, I think you will find her more receptive and wanting to talk."

He said, "I'll try and be here as early as possible."

He gave me a hug and told me how much he loved me and how grateful he was for all I had done for Mom.

On my way to bed, I looked in on Mom. She was asleep. I leaned over, gave her a kiss, and told her I loved her and I would see her in the morning.

Chapter 22

I was abruptly jolted out of a deep sleep by a loud, ringing noise. I looked at the clock; it was 5:30 a.m. I thought, Oh my God! It's the fire alarm! The house is on fire!

I jumped out of bed from a deep sleep and ran toward the door. Halfway there, I noticed that the bell had stopped ringing. Perplexed, I stopped in my tracks and listened for a second and then I heard the ringing again. Then it dawned on me. It was Mom ringing her bell! I began to panic; something must be drastically wrong as she had never used the bell before.

I ran down the stairs as fast as I could, threw open the door, and said "Mom, what's wrong? Are you all right?"

She cried out, "Please! Turn me over. I'm in agony! My hip is killing me!"

As quickly as I could, I lifted her and turned her over on to her left side.

She sighed heavily and said, "That's so much better."

She sank peacefully back onto her pillow, breathing easily. I stood in a daze. I had been in a very deep sleep and I felt shell-shocked. Mom was in a queen-size bed, so I crawled into bed with her and snuggled under the warm comforter close beside her and gently held her hand. It felt so good to be lying next to her.

I closed my eyes and recalled wonderful childhood memories. Many nights I had slept with Mom, and the security and comfort of what that felt like came back to me. I giggled to myself about the times I had woken up in the morning with my feet in Mom's face and my head at the bottom of the bed. How did she put up with me? As I lay there reminiscing, Mom squeezed my hand tightly.

"Mom, your grip is so strong! Where did you get all that strength from?"

She chuckled and said, "I feel good. Why don't you pull up the blinds and get me a drink?"

"Okay, I will."

I opened the blinds to another beautiful fall day. I helped Mom into a sitting position and then went into the kitchen and made a pot of coffee.

I pulled a chair up to Mom's bed and gave her a sip of juice. She was more energetic than I had seen in a long time.

She said, "That coffee smells so good. Could I have a cup?"

Greatly surprised, I said, "Absolutely. I'll get you one."

I wondered, what is going on? She's as clear and strong as she was a month ago.

I brought Mom half a cup of coffee and held it to her lips. She took a few sips and said, "Boy that's tasty. It's been a long time since I've tasted coffee."

Mom's nausea was basically nonexistent now. The few sips of liquid that she consumed daily weren't enough to cause any problems.

Just then, Corky came into the bedroom with his coffee and joined us. He could see improvement in Mom also.

While Corky and Mom were talking, I left the room to call Vern to come visit as quickly as he could because Mom was very talkative, and he would enjoy this time with her. He said that he was just having coffee and would pack up and make sure everything was secure at Mom's house and then would be right over.

I walked back into the room to find Corky and Mom laughing. She was interested in Corky's business, what the kids were doing, and what was happening in our day-to-day lives. Her face lit up when someone said something that pleased her.

Tess and Nigel came in to the room and sat on her bed and held her hand. Nigel stayed a short time only. As Mom said, "Kids get bored: they can't sit around talking for long."

Tess stayed for a while, listening to us chatting and entering into the conversation intermittently. About an hour into our visit, I could see Mom starting to fade. I was anxious; Vern still hadn't arrived.

Corky said, "I'm going to phone Vern again and see what's taking him so long. Anne is starting to lose her concentration, and he's going to miss this opportunity to visit with her while she's so talkative."

Corky came back and said, "Vern's on his way, I sure hope he hurries."

I felt frustrated. I had specifically told him to come early. Why hadn't he tried to get here sooner? I wanted him to experience her lucidity and how much she was like her old self. Unfortunately, by the time Vern arrived, Mom had begun to slip into a dream state again. She was fading rapidly. Vern sat with her for an hour or so, but she wasn't communicating the way she had earlier in the morning. I could see his frustration; he was really having a difficult time with these dramatic changes in Mom. There was so little left of who she used to be, of the mother he knew.

After a time, Vern came out of the bedroom and said, "Mom's not communicating with me at all. She's really in her own world and seems so tired."

"Mom expended a lot of energy this morning. She was really bubbly and talkative, but it was short lived."

"I tried to get here as quickly as I could, but I had to tidy up. I have to go back to Victoria today."

"Are you sure, Vern? Mom has so little time left. She told me she's leaving us today. Can't you stay one more night?"

Vern said, "Listen, Carole. Mom could last another week. We don't know. I have to get back to work. I've missed so much over the last year, and I just can't take any more time off."

I was perturbed, but I understood. In so many ways, I was the lucky one. I could spend as much time as I wanted with Mom, but Vern had to get time off from work and drive seven hours to Vernon and then seven hours back to Victoria.

I believed that Mom was leaving us for good today, and he was certain that I was listening to a delirious woman. He hadn't experienced the conversations that she and I had shared. It was hard for him to understand how Mom could possibly know when she was going to die. So I reluctantly had to say goodbye to Vern. I was puzzled as to how he could leave at such a critical time, with her passage from this world to the next happening any day. I felt sad for him that he was missing out on something so special.

Shortly after Vern had left for Victoria, Corky said to me, "Carole, maybe Vern isn't supposed to be here. This is something that you have to experience, but he doesn't. You have to accept that."

"I guess so, but I still wish he had stayed for at least one more day."

I went into the bedroom to let Mom know that Vern had left. She was very distant.

"I can see that you're really tired, Mom. Can I get you anything?"

"I am tired. I just want to rest." She paused and then said, "Be here tonight at eight. I'm leaving then."

I really didn't know what to say to her, so I said, "Umm okay, uh, do you want the kids and Corky to come at that time too?"

She said with impatience, "Of course I do!"

"Okay Mom, we will all be here. I'll leave you to sleep now."

She didn't respond. She had fallen asleep. She seemed exhausted with the effort it was taking to organize her departure from this world.

I went into the kitchen to talk to Corky.

I said, "Mom told me that she is leaving tonight at eight o'clock. She said this with confidence, and she wants us and the kids in the room with her."

Looking at me intently, he gently said, "Carole, your mom might be wrong. She might be mixed up about this. You do realize that don't you?"

I said, "Yes, I do know that, but Mom has been talking about eight o'clock for the last two weeks. Just the other day, right out of the blue, she asked me again, 'Is it eight o'clock yet?' and I said, 'No Mom, its eleven o'clock in the morning.' All she said was, 'Oh.' This has happened a few times over this last week. I didn't want to make a big deal out of it; I just figured that she had lost track of time with her being so ill."

Corky said, "We will see, but I think you should just go with the flow and not have any preconceived ideas about what could happen.

"Yah, I guess so."

Even though I agreed with Corky, I still had a feeling that Mom clearly knew what she was talking about—even though we didn't. However, I *was* tired of looking like an idiot when I told people what she had been saying about her approaching death. Most of the family thought she was just confused. I, on the other hand, was certain that she knew perfectly well what was happening. She was on a different wavelength than the rest of us, and I was determined to respect what she said all the way to the end. I figured that we would eventually find out who was confused and who wasn't.

৯০

A home care-nurse that we hadn't met before arrived at our house just after two o'clock that afternoon. She offered to sit with Mom for a couple of hours to give me a break, seeing as Mom was the last patient of the day.

I had mixed feelings about leaving Mom's side at such a critical time, but I needed to get out of the house for awhile. My girlfriend Jennifer had invited me out for tea earlier that day, and an hour off was too good to pass up. But instead of tea, we went and had a big bowl of vanilla ice cream.

When we were settled in our booth, savoring our ice cream, Jennifer began, "Carole, I have learned so much from your family about the process of dying and so have my kids. We talk a lot about what's happening to your mom. Having watched you and your mom over these months, death seems a little less scary now. The way your mom talks about her death is so enlightening and comforting. I really am so lucky to have had this experience with both of you."

I said, "Yes, it's changed my life too. It's hard to believe that she will be gone soon, but I feel sure that she will be just fine. I'm the one that's not going to do so well. Even though she is so sick, I can still hold her hand and I can still touch her. Soon I won't be able to do any of those things, and that's going to be very difficult for me."

"At least you've had this last year with her."

"Yes, many people have said that it won't be as hard when she dies because I've had this year to mourn and prepare for her death.

189

But somehow, I don't think it's going to be any easier. I'm still going to miss her terribly."

Jennifer said, "I can't imagine losing my mom. I would feel like you too. It wouldn't matter how much preparation I had, I would still be devastated."

We talked awhile longer and then Jennifer drove me home.

ès ø

I walked into Mom's room to find the nurse sitting quietly beside Mom's bed. I whispered to her, "How has Mom been?"

"Your mom's been sleeping most of the time. She's very peaceful."

Mom opened her eyes and said ever so softly, "Hi sweetie."

I sat on the bed holding her hand.

"Hi Mom, how are you doing?" I asked.

Mom smiled weakly, "I'm finally on my way. I'm going home tonight," she whispered.

"I know Mom, and we'll all be here with you, so don't worry."

"Good." She said.

I thought to myself, this poor nurse probably thinks we're half mad talking like this. The regular nurses over the last month had experienced much of Mom's journey home, but this nurse must have wondered about us. But at this point, it didn't matter; I just wanted to make Mom feel comfortable by talking about what was important to her.

It was time for the nurse to leave. As she was packed up her things, I told her I didn't need an evening nurse. I could handle things on my own. She told me to call if I needed help, and a nurse would come at anytime.

I made an early dinner. I really wanted to spend as much time with Mom as I could before eight o'clock. Even though everyone thought I was crazy, I really did believe she was leaving tonight, so by five thirty that evening I was sitting by her bed, stroking her hand.

With a lump in my throat and tears on my cheeks, I told her how much I loved her and how much I was going to miss her. I told her

190

what a wonderful mother she had been and that I knew how much she loved me; and in the whole scheme of things, that was all that mattered.

Her replies were short, and she mostly answered by saying, "I know."

She spoke with her eyes closed, and the few times she did open them, her eyes were glazed and seemed to look right through me.

Many mixed emotions were churning inside me. As I sat quietly beside her, I pondered what life would be like without her. I was losing that unconditional love that only a parent has for a child. She had always been there for me. If I was down, or sad, or didn't feel good about myself or my life, I could call Mom. She always had the right things to say, and even those times when I didn't want to burden her with my problems, just knowing she was there always gave me the strength to get through the hard times.

This last year had shown me how much she had done for me and how important she was in my life. I saw how I had taken our relationship for granted. I was often too busy or too caught up in my own life to acknowledge how important she was to me. If only I could go back to some of those times I had put Mom last when I should have put her first. But sadly I knew there was no going back, and soon she would be gone forever.

Chapter 23

It was a few minutes before eight in the evening. Mom's breathing was heavy and ragged. She responded only if I talked loudly and repeated her name a few times, and even then, her response was very limited.

At eight sharp, I called Corky and the kids into the room as she had requested.

Tess sat on the bed and held her grandma's hand. I sat by the bed, and Corky stood by the door, with his arms folded. Nigel stood at the edge of the bed and said, "How long do we have to stay here Mom?"

I said, "I'm not sure. All I know is that Grandma wants us to be here at this time." We waited in silence, looking at Mom. None of us really knew what to do or say, or, for that matter, what Mom had in store for us.

After fifteen minutes or so, Nigel said, "Mom, can I go and play my game, please?"

I knew he was not comfortable with what was happening, so I said, "Go ahead, Nigel. We'll call you if anything happens."

He was so glad to get out of the bedroom and back to his game. I asked Tess if she would like to leave the room, but she said she wanted to stay.

Mom lay with her eyes closed.

Suddenly she opened her eyes wide, looked outward, and started yelling, "Come! Come quickly! Hurry, Hurry!"

She wasn't talking to any of us. She seemed to be talking to someone we couldn't see.

As she was yelling, she began to panic. She turned to look at me wide-eyed and said, "Help me please! Help me, I'm lost!"

This was similar to what had occurred the other day, but this time I had more understanding as to what was happening. I said, "Ask for help, Mom. Mom, you're okay; you're safe, just ask for help."

Her body began to move involuntarily. It was as if she was on a roller-coaster ride, and she made sounds like 'oh, oh, oh!"

As quickly as this all began, it was over. She became calm and quiet again and returned to her heavy breathing.

We looked at each other in wonder. We left the bedroom and went into the kitchen to talk.

I asked Corky, "What do you think is happening? I remember reading about this. There were examples of people very close to death who would point and reach out to thin air. This can be a sign that death is close, and I think that's now happening to Mom."

As we were talking, we could hear Mom yelling from the bedroom.

"Hurry up, come and get me!"

For some reason, we found the way she was talking to be humorous. We knew this was a grave time and we shouldn't find this funny, but I think we were so baffled that this was the only way we could react to what was going on. We couldn't help but laugh.

I said, "She really wants out of here now!"

Corky and I went back into Mom's room and found her composed again. Her breathing was labored, and her eyes were closed.

I tried to talk to her, but she wouldn't respond.

"Corky, we should get her ready for the night. Can you lift her, and I'll fix her pillows?"

Corky tried to pull her up, but her body was completely rigid. It was as if she had seized up.

He said, "This is really strange. She's as stiff as a board. I can hardly move her."

Corky secured his arms around her and said in a firm voice, "Okay Anne, I'm going to pull you up now."

Mom opened her eyes but obviously had no control over her body. Corky managed to get her into what appeared to be a fairly comfortable position. A few minutes later, the kids came into the room and gave Grandma a kiss and said good night.

Tess asked, "Mom, do you think Grandma is going to die tonight?"

I said, "Sweetie, I don't know. We will just have to wait and see what happens."

She looked sad, and said, "I think Grandma is going to leave, Mom. I think she will go tonight."

I gave her a hug and said, "Remember, Grandma always said that she would be with you. She'll never be that far away."

She said, "I know." Pausing, she said, "Night, Mom. I love you."

I stayed in Mom's room while Corky put the kids to bed. Again, with her arms reaching out for something or someone, she began to shout, "Hurry. Hurry! Quickly! Quickly!"

Wow, I thought, she *really* does want to get out of here.

She had completely disconnected from us now. At that point, I just wished she would leave. She had suffered enough.

It was nine-thirty when I asked her if she wanted her sleeping pill. I had to call her name several times to get a response.

Finally in a forced voice she said, "Yes." It seemed it take every ounce of energy to speak that one word.

I put the sleeping pill into her mouth. I tried to give her a sip of water, but she was oblivious to everything I was doing. The pill just sat on her tongue and began melting. It must have tasted bitter, but she didn't seem to notice. I took the pill out of her mouth as it didn't seem she needed it anyway. She was far too busy dying and off somewhere else to really care.

I was exhausted. Here it was close to ten o'clock, and she was still hanging on.

I wondered how much longer this was going to continue, and why she wouldn't let go?

I couldn't take it anymore. I was definitely agitated. I stomped out to the kitchen to find Corky. He was standing by the sink, getting a glass of water.

With a lot of frustration and irritation, I loudly said, "Why won't she die? She said she was leaving at eight o'clock, and here it is ten o'clock and she's still alive! I can't do this anymore. I've had it!"

Corky said, "Carole, she'll go when she's ready. Maybe it's like going on a trip. Your flight is at eight o'clock, but there is still the journey to get to your destination. It's like she is en route now.

I retorted angrily, "Well she should have told me that!"

I took a few deep breaths; I calmed myself and thought about what Corky had just said.

I responded, "I guess that does make sense. She knew she was boarding the flight at eight. The words she used was that she was leaving, not dying. Maybe she knew that after eight she wouldn't be able to talk to us anymore." I paused, "You know, the more that I think about it, the more I believe that what you are saying could be right."

I paused. "Do you remember me telling you about a dream I had a couple of weeks ago? It was the dream where I was driving Mom across this wide, long bridge over water to get to the other side. At the end of the bridge, there was a gate keeper. He came out of his hut and put his hand up for me to stop the car. He told me I couldn't go any farther, only Mom could. I was told to drop her off, but I wasn't allowed to stay with her. So maybe she is crossing the bridge right now, and we are helping her to get to the other side."

Corky said, "I do remember you telling me. That was such a profound dream."

I went back into Mom's room. She was breathing very heavily and was completely unaware of my presence. She was very busy dying, and seeing her like this I knew it was over. She said she was dying tonight, and it was obvious the end was near.

I don't know what made me decide to go up to bed and not stay with her until she passed away. Maybe I just couldn't face the inevitable. I couldn't face the end. I crawled into bed in sheer exhaustion and deep mourning. I dreaded waking up tomorrow.

Chapter 24

I was suddenly awoken in the night. I groggily peered at the clock; it was 11:12 p.m. The first thought that came to my mind was that Mom had died. The second thought was, if I check on Mom now and she is gone, I will have to do something about it.

What I really didn't want to admit was that I was afraid to go in and find her dead. I needed a good night's sleep to do that. I needed time.

In the middle of all these conflicting thoughts, I fell asleep and didn't wake up again until the alarm went off in the morning. I sat up in bed and braced myself. I just knew that she had died, and I had to prepare myself for what I was about to find. I quietly walked down the stairs and stood at her door.

I put my hand on the doorknob, paused, and took a deep breath. I hesitated. I didn't know if I could handle finding her dead, yet I knew I had no choice but to go into the room. I opened the door.

For a split second, I felt relief with a tinge of optimism. She's still alive I thought.

She was in the same position I had left her in the night before. The distinct difference now was that the room was completely silent; there were no sounds of breathing. I walked over to the side of the bed and reached for her hand with hope. I hoped that somehow she would still be alive. I softly touched her skin; it felt cool.

The room was dark, so I drew up the blinds part way to let light into the room. I turned toward Mom and saw that she had the most beautiful, radiant smile on her face. Her eyes were open and she was looking up and outward. I marveled at this incredible sight.

With a choked voice, I whispered, "Well Mom, you made it. You're finally free."

My throat and chest were aching, but I knew I couldn't cry. I had to keep my emotions in check. I had to get the kids off to school before I would let the dam break.

Maybe I should tell the kids when they get up that their Grandma has passed away, I wondered. But on second thought, I decided no: I need time to collect myself.

I knew the kids would be devastated when they found out that she was gone, and the state I was in, I wouldn't be able to comfort them. I was hurting too much. I would tell them after school.

I turned away from the bed, walked out of the room, and closed the door.

I woke the kids for school and began making breakfast. As I buttered Nigel's toast, it was sinking in that my whole world had just changed. Mom was gone forever. My chest was aching so intensely that I thought it was going to explode; it took every ounce of courage to control myself from completely breaking down.

As I continued making breakfast, I began to feel intense heat on my upper back and across my shoulders, as if someone had laid a heating pad on me. I stopped what I was doing and closed my eyes, savoring this powerful sensation. I wanted to keep this moment alive; I knew intuitively that it was Mom putting her arm around my shoulders to comfort me.

Nigel snapped me out of deep thought.

"Mom, did you put peanut butter on my toast?"

I barely responded, "Yes, I did." I turned to give Nigel his toast, and the sensation was gone.

We sat down at the table to eat our breakfast together. Tess said urgently, "Mom, you'd better go and check on Grandma."

"I will Tess, but I'll wait until you guys go to school."

"No Mom, I want you to check on her now."

"I promise I'll go in after you go to school. I don't want to disturb her right now."

I was trying not to lie, but I also didn't want her to know that Mom had passed on. In that moment, she seemed to be satisfied with my response, so the two of them went off to school with Corky. I was so glad they got out the door earlier than usual as I wasn't sure I could hold on much longer.

છ્જ

After they left, I burst into tears, sobbing. I had lost her and now she was gone. Waves of grief overcame me. The intensity of pain in my heart was beyond my comprehension as I wept from the depth of my being. I cried until there was no emotion left; only numbness embraced me as I sat silently in complete physical, mental, and emotional exhaustion.

I had to collect myself; there was so much I had to do and so many people I had to call.

Dr. Morgan had asked me to call him as soon as Mom died because he wanted to be the person to pronounce her passing. I wiped my tears, took a deep breath, phoned his answering service, and asked for him to call me as soon as possible. I hung up, took another deep breath and then dialed my brother.

I thought, Poor guy. He just got home late last night, and now he's going to have to turn around and come back again.

"Hi, it's me."

There was a pause, and then Vern said, "She died, didn't she? I just knew it when the phone rang. I knew you were going to tell me that."

I said, "Yes Vern, she did."

There was silence, and then he asked, "What time do you think she died?"

"I think it was last night, around eleven o'clock. I might be wrong, but I'm sure we'll be able to find out."

"Well, I guess I'd better arrange time off work right away. I know this isn't the best time to talk about it, but when do you think we should have Mom's funeral?"

"I don't know. Most people usually have it three to four days after death. I guess Thursday would be a good day, except that's Remembrance Day, November 11, and I don't know if that is an appropriate day to have a funeral."

"I would really appreciate holding off as long as we can. I can't make it to Vernon until Wednesday, so Thursday would work best for me. That will give me some time to wrap up some work here."

"Okay, I will ask at the funeral home whether or not Remembrance Day is appropriate."

He asked, "Are you doing okay?"

"I'm doing as well as can be expected, I guess. I feel dazed right now."

"You hang in there, Carole. We'll get there on Wednesday to help you with the preparations for the funeral."

I said, "The call alert on my phone is beeping. I have to go; it's probably the doctor. I'll call you back."

I hung up and went to my other line. It was Dr. Morgan.

With a lump in my throat, I said, "Hello Dr. Morgan. Mom passed on in the night, and you had said to call you."

Dr. Morgan paused and gently said, "Oh, I'm so sorry that she is gone. How are you doing Carole?"

"I'm handling it."

"I know how difficult this is. I am on my way. I'll see you within the next half an hour."

I hung up and walked back into Mom's room. I held her hand and began to cry. I walked over to the other side of the bed and lay down beside her. I put my arm around her waist and my head on her chest and hugged her. She was gone. I'd never hear her voice again, and I'd never feel her arms around me again.

This was going to be the last time I would be able to be with her.

As I hugged Mom, I thought about how she had known when she was going to die. She was right; she did go home on the day that she had said. I was so thankful that I had listened to her. She was now in a good place—in that wonderful place she had joyfully described.

I was certain she was finally at peace and free from all that pain, but it was the opposite for me; now I was the one in pain. I didn't think it would hurt this much. I knew instinctively that it was going to take a long time before I would heal from this loss.

I began feeling pangs of guilt. I hadn't really wanted her to die last night; I just couldn't bear seeing her suffer anymore and I couldn't handle the responsibility anymore. I began sobbing uncontrollably. I had such a feeling of emptiness and despair.

I lay with her until the doorbell rang. I collected myself, blew my nose, put on a good face, and answered the door to Dr. Morgan.

He put his hand on my shoulder and said, "No matter how much notice we have, when we lose a loved one, it's still hard isn't it?"

All I could do was nod my head in agreement and point to Mom's room. Walking into her room, he abruptly stopped by her bed, and sounding surprised said, "My God, she has a beautiful smile on her face!"

He turned and looked at me in amazement and said, "What a peaceful, wonderful way she has died."

Again, I just nodded my head, agreeing. It took everything in me to stop from bursting into tears. I turned and walked into the living room to wait until he had finished with Mom.

When he was done, he came into the living room and asked, "Did she die in the night?"

"I think she must have died around eleven last night. I woke up briefly around that time and felt that she was gone."

"Well, her skin is cool, so it may well have been before midnight. The coroner will be able to calculate close to the time she passed. He paused and quietly said, "You can phone the funeral home anytime you like. You don't have to have your mom taken away today. It's quite alright for her to stay here at your home for a few days."

I said, "I don't really know what I'll do right now. This is all so overwhelming at the moment."

As I walked him to the door, he turned and said, "Your mother was a very fortunate woman to die so peacefully. She was lucky to have you."

I said, "Thank you, but really, I was the lucky one. Mom gave me the opportunity to know what death holds for us and how extraordinary it can be. She gave our family a great gift, and the gift was not to fear death. It seems that the afterlife is more wonderful than we can imagine. I am truly thankful for this experience."

He smiled and walked outside and said, "If you require anything, please call me. I'm here if you need me."

"Thank you, I will."

ॐ ॐ

Even though I could keep Mom at home for a few days longer, I didn't have the need to do this. I wanted the kids to remember her as the healthy, vibrant grandmother that she had been over the years. I felt that seeing Mom when she was dead, even though she was smiling, would be hard for the kids. So with that decision made, I phoned the funeral home. I told them that Mom had passed away and that the doctor had been to the house and had pronounced her passing. The secretary said that the coroner would be right over. I hung up the phone and walked back into Mom's room, but this time I didn't stay for long. I kissed her on the cheek, touched her hair, pulled the covers up to her chin, and walked out of the room.

I wasn't sure what to do with myself while I waited for the coroner, so I decided to go into the kitchen to clean up the morning mess. I walked over to the sink and looked out the window at the beautiful fall colors. My eyes feasted on the brilliant orange and yellow leaves. I found myself drifting into deep thought.

Finally it was over, and the burden had been lifted from my shoulders. I had been so wrapped up with Mom's life this last year that I had forgotten my own. I now had to carry on without her. Mom was finally free, and I was finally free. I had thought that I would feel better, but instead I felt worse. Nothing could have prepared me for the grief I was feeling or how much I already missed her. I still had so much I wanted to say to her.

I felt overwhelming guilt that I had been so impatient last night. Why couldn't I have held up for a few more hours? Why didn't I sit with her until she passed over? I felt deep sadness and regret that I didn't stay until the very end.

Looking down at the kitchen counter, my thoughts returned to the clutter around me. I began washing the frying pan. As I looked up from the sink, I saw the black van from the funeral home pull up

201

in front of our garage. Two men in long black overcoats got out of the van and began walking toward the house. I grabbed the dish towel, and while I was drying my hands, I walked to the back door. I began to wonder, why do people who deal with the dead always dress so morbidly? These guys really need to brighten up their wardrobes; they look like characters straight out of the *The Matrix*.

I opened the door. The two men stood in front of me with their heads bowed and their hands folded in front of them. They politely introduced themselves, and then the coroner softly asked me where my mother was. I guided them to the bedroom, but this time I didn't go in. They quietly slipped into her room and tip-toed around, whispering to each other from time to time. A few moments went by before they came out of her room. The coroner said he would be taking Mom to the funeral home right away.

I nodded my head and then turned and walked into the living room, sat on the couch, and stared out the window.

A few moments passed without a sound until I saw them bring a stretcher into Mom's room. I could hear them whispering again in hushed tones. I wondered how they would be transporting her to the funeral home, and then I heard the scraping of the zipper.

Oh my God, I realized, they're putting her in a body bag! It made me shudder as the tingles went up my spine.

It seemed to be such a cold-hearted thing to do. I wished then that I had gone outside while they were doing this. I wished I hadn't heard that sound. I started to cry again. It was so final; I would never see her again. I didn't want to watch them take her away. I kept staring out the window until I knew they had put her in the van.

The coroner came back and said, "We will take good care of your mother, so please don't worry. He paused and said, "There is something I need you to do as soon as you can. Could you please bring some clothes to dress your mom for the cremation?"

I said, "Okay. I'll bring her clothes to the funeral home tomorrow, if that's all right. Do you know when they will do the cremation?"

The coroner said, "It will probably be late tomorrow or the next day."

I said goodbye and closed the door. I immediately went into Mom's room, turned the light on, and opened the blinds as wide as I could. It seemed so empty; it just didn't seem right that she wasn't there. I was filled with nervous energy, so I began cleaning up. I stripped the bed, washed Mom's clothes, and put her things in boxes. When I had finished, you wouldn't have known that someone had just died in the room. I don't know why I was in such a hurry to clear everything away. Maybe I didn't want to be reminded that she was gone, or maybe I just wanted an excuse to be doing something so I didn't have to cry anymore.

I finally sat down with a cup of coffee, when the phone rang. It was Tess on the line.

"Mom how is Grandma? I can't stop thinking about her. Is she okay?" She asked.

I didn't want to lie to her, but I wasn't going to tell her on the phone that her Grandma had died. I knew that I still needed more time to digest everything and grieve alone. I wasn't composed enough to be able to comfort her or Nigel in their grief.

"Tess, Grandma is just fine."

"Mom, did Grandma die?"

"Tess, don't worry about Grandma. You just have a good day, and we'll see you after school."

She hesitated and then said, "Okay. Bye, Mom. I love you."

I hung up. I felt bad that I had lied to her. Her intuition was telling her that her Grandma had died, and she wanted me to confirm her feelings. I felt guilty that I had not told her, but I didn't want to tell her over the phone.

Corky phoned and asked, "How are you doing? Do you want me to come home?"

"No, I'm okay. I need to be alone right now. I need some time to sort out my feelings. Tess phoned at lunch time, and I told her Mom was fine. I guess on one level it wasn't really a lie. I'm sure Mom is just fine right now."

Corky said, "Are you sure you don't want me to come home? Are you sure you're okay?"

"Really, I'm fine Corky. I just need some time on my own."

"Okay. You don't have to worry about the kids after school. Archie will pick them up at three o'clock and bring them home."

"That will help me a lot. I really don't feel like facing anyone right now. I look a mess."

Three o'clock came around quickly. I rehearsed over and over in my mind what I was going to tell the kids. I wondered how they were going to take her death. I wanted to protect them from the pain that I was feeling, but I knew that would be impossible.

Tess would be hit the hardest. She had held many of her feelings inside over the last year about her Grandma being ill, and I was worried about her reaction to the news that I had to give her.

It was three-fifteen and the kids would be home any minute. I hoped I wouldn't cry when I gave them this sad news.

The kids came running into the house with Archie and found me sitting in the living room. They both looked at me and Nigel said, "Mom, you look like you've been crying."

Oh God, I thought, I have to tell them now. A big lump was forming in my throat as I said, "Come here you guys, and sit with me." I put my arms around them and held them close. With a shaky voice, I said, "Grandma died last night. She is finally free of her sick body." I paused, "I am sure she is in a wonderful place now." I choked back my tears.

The kids sat quietly for a long moment. Tess started to cry. I held her tight and said, "It's okay, Tess. Grandma will always be with you. She's just in a different place."

She cried, "I want to see Grandma!" She bent over, sobbing her little heart out.

As I held her and rocked her, I said, "I know, I do too. Oh Tess honey, it's all right. Everything will be all right."

Tess sobbed for a few moments longer, and then after calming down, she looked down at the carpet with tears running down her cheeks. I knew that the next few months were going to be very difficult for her.

I turned to Nigel. I was surprised at his reaction. He had tears in his eyes, but he didn't appear to be as upset.

He looked up at me with his big green eyes and asked, "What do you think Grandma is doing right now?"

"Well, I think that Grandma is right here in this room, watching all of us and probably trying to tell us not to be sad because she is finally free."

"I think that she is really happy now, Mom. She doesn't have her broken body anymore."

I smiled and thought how profound Nigel was and how he had such a wonderful way of looking at life for such a young boy.

"Nigel, I think you are right."

Archie sat silently across the room with tears in his eyes. He said, "I'm so sorry that she is gone. We are all going to miss her so much."

He came over and gave the kids and me a warm hug. The tears were flowing from us all. Our hearts were aching together.

☜☞

Evening came, and I was exhausted. I had spent over an hour phoning Mom's close friends with the news of Mom's passing. Some of her friends were so upset that they could barely say goodbye to me.

By the time the kids were ready to go to bed, I was so drained that I could barely tuck them in for the night.

I sat with Nigel for a short time on his bed. He seemed to be handling Mom's death much better than I thought. He was quite certain that Grandma was just fine. I wondered if he was hiding his feelings, but I knew not to pressure him. I was sure that his feelings of grief would eventually come out.

Nigel gave me a big kiss and a hug and said very intensely, "Mom, don't worry about Grandma. She's here right now, and she's really happy."

Chuckling, I ran my fingers through his hair, leaned over, and kissed his cheek. "I know, Nigel. I'm sure she's very happy now. You know so much about life for your few short years. Love you, sleep tight."

I walked into Tess's room to find her very upset and lying on her bed crying.

With deep sadness in her voice she said, "I miss Grandma so much. I wish she hadn't died."

My heart was breaking for her. What could I say to take her pain away? I held her as she sobbed.

She said, "Grandma should never have smoked. Why didn't she stop?"

I said, "She wanted to, but she had smoked for so many years that it was difficult for her to quit."

Stroking Tess's hair, I said, "Grandma's much better now because she's out of that body that caused her so much pain. And who knows, Grandma could come to you in many different ways, maybe even in your dreams. I would like to think that we will see her again. Life is a mystery."

I said, "Close your eyes and go to sleep. It's been a hard day for you, and sleep heals many things."

"It won't heal Grandma. She's not coming back."

I said softly, "I know, Tess. It's going to take time to heal from this. I love you, sleep tight."

I walked into the bathroom and looked at myself in the mirror. I looked exhausted; I was emotionally, mentally, and physically worn out. In that instant, Mom's adage on the plane crossed my mind. I began to chuckle and said out loud, "I look like I've been dragged through a hedge backwards!" Not only did I look like that, I felt like that.

I finally crawled into bed, curled up on my side, and put the quilt over my head. Lying in the dark, my mind was on Mom. I wondered where she might be right now. I remembered reading that shortly after death, people often come to say goodbye to their loved ones. My mind went back to last night. Why did I awaken around eleven o'clock? Was that Mom trying to say goodbye to me?

I had a lot of regret over the way I had handled last night. I should have stayed with her in her room until she died, or at the very least I should have gotten up when I had awakened at eleven. Why didn't

I? I was mad at myself for not being more aware and tuned in. I had a feeling that I would be sorry for my actions for a long time.

It only took a few minutes before I was asleep, and the next thing I knew it was morning.

≈≪

I had planned to let the kids sleep in, but they were already awake and out of bed. I offered them the chance to stay home from school, but to my surprise, both of them decided that they would go. I had mixed feelings about this. On one hand, I was worried that they might break down and I wouldn't be there to console them; yet on the other hand, maybe this was the way they wanted to process their grandma's death. I let them make their own decision and told them to phone me at any time if they felt bad, and I would come and pick them up immediately.

I stood at the kitchen window and waved goodbye to the kids as they walked to Corky's truck. I thought how brave, strong, and resilient they were.

Corky phoned around ten o'clock and said, "I'm just reminding you about the appointment we have with the funeral home at eleven thirty. Can you be ready by then?"

"Yes, I can. Thanks for organizing this for me. There isn't much time to plan the funeral so we have to get on with it."

He said, "I'm sure it's the last thing in the world you want to do right now, but we don't have much of a choice."

"I know. It'll be good to get it over with. I'll be ready when you pick me up. See you then."

Cheryl phoned shortly after I hung up the phone.

She asked, "How are you doing Carole? You must be feeling pretty rough, eh?"

"I'm better than I was yesterday. I think I'm too busy to really have time to feel sorry for myself." I took a deep breath and continued, "I have to go to the funeral home this morning and make plans for Mom's funeral."

"You're going to need help. What can I do for you?"

207

"Well, I need to go to Mom's house later today to get cups and saucers and some of her clothes for the funeral. Would you have time to help me?"

"Sure. No problem. Does one thirty work for you?"

"That would be perfect. See you then."

߬‧镡

Corky and I arrived at the funeral home right on time. We walked into a dimly lit foyer with ornate, dark brown wood paneling throughout. It was so quiet that you could have easily heard a pin drop. Within a minute, the funeral director came around the corner to greet us. I could not help but think how closely he resembled the two men that had come to collect Mom. He was wearing a black suit and had a very somber look on his face.

As we were walking down the hall, I thought about what a tough job funeral directors had, dealing with death and sorrow day in and day out. I wondered how many years someone could do this kind of work without becoming depressed.

We went into his office and sat in the chairs facing his desk. The funeral director asked us what we wanted to do to celebrate Mom's life.

I said, "Well, Mom had clearly specified that she wanted her service to be in the United Church, and we would like to abide by her wishes."

The funeral director and Corky both felt that the church was too large and that it could feel empty. They said that the chapel here at the funeral home would be better suited for the service. I thought for a moment about what they were suggesting. Because Mom's illness had ended any kind of opportunity to create a social life in Vernon, I wasn't sure how many people would come. I felt torn about changing what she had wished for, but I reluctantly had to agree; it was a very large church.

With that decision made, we gave him a list of Mom's requests for her Celebration of Life service. We told him we wanted someone to play the bagpipes at the beginning and at the end of the service. We wanted two songs sung by a soprano. The first song was to be "All My Trials, Lord Soon Be Over" and the second, "Amazing Grace." Mom had wanted Reverend Brian Jones to officiate at the service. The funeral director was very accommodating and was willing to do anything we wanted.

Just as we were saying goodbye, a question about Mom's death came to mind.

I asked, "Do you happen to know what time Mom died? Dr. Morgan told me that the coroner would know."

The funeral director said, "Yes we do. Your mom died somewhere between eleven and eleven thirty in the evening, on November 8.

I thanked him and with the details for the service arranged, we left the funeral home.

In the van on the way home, Corky said, "It's really amazing; Anne *did* know the day she was going to die. You know, what's really extraordinary is the only day available this week is November 11, Remembrance Day, for your mom's funeral. In so many ways, it's a perfect day what with Leif dying in the war and Anne telling us that he was coming to take her home. When you really think about it, the day of her funeral couldn't have been planned better if you tried."

I said, "It's actually quite bizarre when you think about it. I don't think you could plan that even if you did try."

Corky said, "I know, it's extremely bizarre. But like I said, in the whole scheme of things, it really couldn't be a more perfect day for Anne's funeral."

�� ��

Cheryl arrived on time to drive me to Mom's house to pick up the china and her clothes for the funeral. I was glad Cheryl was with me as I did not relish going into the house alone. I unlocked the door to a cold and lifeless space. I quickly found the thermostat and turned up the heat. The furnace came on with a rumble. I stood in the living room, looking around at the countless memories from my childhood: so many photographs of our family together. I felt bitter in that moment. She died too young.

209

I forced myself out of these thoughts and said to Cheryl, "I guess we had better get busy."

We opened the china cabinet doors to dozens of cups, saucers, and teapots that Mom had collected over the years. She always loved fine china and crystal, and she had plenty of it. We packed up the items that would be useful for the reception and carried the boxes out to the car. Walking back into Mom's house, I dreaded the next chore I had ahead of me. The hardest part was yet to come; I had to go into Mom's closet and find appropriate clothing for her to wear for the cremation.

Tentatively, I walked towards Mom's closet, took a deep breath, opened the door, and did what I had to do. I chose a dark fuchsia suit, white silk blouse, and black high heels that Mom had loved. I was told that she would be dressed perfectly, right down to her stockings. I went to her dresser, opened the drawer, and found many pairs of neatly folded nylons. As I was taking a new pair out of the drawer, I was reminded of a story that Mom had told me. Nylons were virtually impossible to get in London during the war, so she used to draw a black line up the back of her leg to look like she was wearing stockings. She said all the girls did that.

The scent of Mom's things brought me back into the room. This was so difficult: the clothes smelled like her, and her favorite perfume was still lingering. I really didn't want to stay there any longer; too much of her was all around me. My chest began to tighten. I was overwhelmed, and I had to leave.

ಸಲ⊷

The next two days went by in a whirl; there was so much to organize for Mom's funeral. Archie arranged for the Pythian Sisters, a service club in town, to host the reception at our house after the funeral. The ladies would make and serve sandwiches, cakes, cookies, tea and coffee. This was all done by donation.

It seemed that the doorbell never stopped ringing with delivery people bringing bouquets of flowers and cards. Phone calls came regularly from people giving their condolences and offering their help with anything that our family might need. I was so grateful for the love and support we received.

In many ways, planning for Mom's funeral was a blessing. It kept me busy and took my mind off how much I missed her. Only when I put my head on the pillow at night would I mourn and feel her loss.

Chapter 25

Vern and Sandy arrived at our house late Wednesday afternoon along with my nephew whom we always called little Vern—except he was not so little anymore. He was twenty-four years old and over six-feet tall. He had grown up to be a remarkable person, and Mom had been very proud him.

I wondered how my brother was dealing with the loss of Mom. He had always been good at hiding his feelings, but this time it was easy for me to see what he was feeling under that composed exterior. I could see the deep sadness in his eyes.

Sandy and I finished up the last of the details in readiness for the funeral the next day. At dinner, we reminisced, laughed, and cried about our life with Mom.

Just as we were digging into our dessert, Vern said, "I can't believe she was smiling when she died; that is so amazing. She had such a peaceful death."

He paused, looked down at his dessert, and quietly said, "It's too bad I wasn't there when she died, but that's the way it had to be, I guess."

I could see that he felt bad about not being with her in the last hours of her life. I wanted to console him.

I said, "It doesn't matter. You were here for Mom when she most needed you, and you were here for me when I needed you. That's all that counts. We both really appreciated that. It was impossible to talk with her near the end, anyway. She was very busy dying and didn't want to be bothered by anything at all."

Vern said, "Thanks for telling me that. I want to remember all the good things with Mom now. We were pretty lucky to have had her as a mom. Our childhood wasn't perfect, but all in all it was really good. She really tried to be a good mom, and as far as I'm concerned, she was the best mom anyone could have."

Sandy said, "Your mom always made me feel that I was a part of the family. I really felt like she was my mom too."

"Yes, she thought of you as a daughter." I said.

We were silent for a moment, and then I said, "I hope Mom's funeral goes well. I'm really not up for this at all. I feel guilty saying this, but I'm looking forward to tomorrow being over with."

Vern said, "Yah, funerals are never easy, but don't worry. I think we've got everything covered."

Vern turned to Sandy and said, "I'm tired. Are you ready to go?"

After Vern and Sandy left for Mom's house, I quickly cleaned up the kitchen and then fell into bed. Tomorrow was going to be a big day: a big day that I dreaded in so many ways.

∂∞◆

I woke up thinking about what loomed ahead of me. I didn't feel like going to Mom's funeral. I wasn't up to facing a large group of people, and I didn't feel like socializing. The last thing I wanted to do was weep in front of everyone. I crossed my fingers, hoping that I could greet my friends and Mom's friends without crying.

Reluctantly, I got out of bed and jumped into the shower. I hoped that the hot water would be revitalizing, but as I walked back into the bedroom, all I wanted to do was crawl into bed and pull the covers over my head. I was exhausted and I dreaded the thought of having to deal with more emotional upheaval and sadness, but I didn't have a choice. I had to keep going for one more day. I walked over to the closet and put on a pair of sweat pants and a t-shirt and went downstairs to make coffee.

It was going to be a busy morning with the caterer arriving early to prepare for the reception. I looked at the time and realized that they would be arriving any moment, and sure enough, just as I began buttering my toast, four elderly ladies close to my mother's age knocked at our door.

They came into the kitchen in a whirl. As they rushed around the kitchen busily making sandwiches and cutting cakes, it brought back memories of my childhood. I was reminded that Mom had also belonged to a service club for many years and had donated countless volunteer hours to raise money for local projects and for people in need, and these ladies were doing the same thing.

As I was pouring myself a cup of coffee, one of the ladies said to me, "Now dear, don't you worry about the tea arrangements, we will take care of everything including serving the guests. You just relax and take it easy."

"Thank you so much. You have no idea how much I appreciate your help today." I said.

Having these ladies take over the details for the reception was a huge relief. The last thing I needed was to worry about organizing the reception. These ladies were taking a big load off my shoulders.

I walked out of the kitchen and found Corky sitting in the living room.

I said, "You know, these women are very special. They are so generous and charitable. I wonder what's going to happen when this generation all pass on. I wonder if service clubs will continue to thrive in the future."

He said, "I know. It's so important that we keep this tradition going."

The doorbell rang. Vern, Sandy, and Vern Jr. arrived at the house, ready for the funeral. Sandy looked elegant in her white suit, while I was still in my sweat pants. I was having trouble deciding on what to wear.

"Sandy, I have two suits and I don't know which one to choose. Can you help me?"

"Sure," she said. "Let's go upstairs and have a look."

We rifled through my closet and chose a royal blue suit jacket with a black skirt.

Sandy said, "This is perfect. You'll look great in this."

"Alright," I said. "That's what I'll wear."

I paused for a moment and then asked, "Sandy, could you sit with me for a moment? I have something I want to give to you."

We sat down on the bed, and I began, "Mom was wearing three rings when she passed away. Two of the rings are very similar; they are both blue sapphires."

As I handed Sandy one of the rings, I said, "I know that Mom would have wanted you to have this blue sapphire ring. It will give you something to remember her by."

Sandy looked at me with gratitude and began to cry.

She said, "Oh Carole, I will cherish this forever. You don't know how much this means to me, and I will never take it off. Whenever I look at this ring, I will think of your mom."

We hugged each other for a moment, and then found a tissue to dry our eyes.

I looked at my watch. It was getting late, and I needed to get ready for the funeral. As I was rushing around getting dressed, I wondered how the kids were doing.

Just as I walked out of the bedroom, Tess called me. I walked in to her room to find her sitting on the edge of her bed, looking down at her dangling feet.

"Mom, I don't want to go to the funeral." She looked up at me and asked, "Do I have to go?"

I knew why she didn't want to go. This wasn't the first family funeral she had been to in recent years.

I said, "Yes sweetie, you have to go. Grandma would want you there."

"I hate funerals. They make me feel so bad."

I didn't know what to say. I felt sad that the kids had to go to yet another funeral. Two of their grandparents had died the year before: my dad and Corky's mom. They had both died within a month of each other, and the loss had been overwhelming for the family.

"Tess, I know how you feel because I don't want to go either. I wish this was all over, but it's important that we say goodbye. It's important to get together with our family and friends and celebrate Grandma's life. I know this is hard for you, but it will be over soon, and then, hopefully, we can put all of this to rest and move on."

She put her arms around my waist and hugged me and said, "I know Mom. I'll go, but I don't want to."

"It's okay honey. It will be over soon."

❧◈

We arrived at the funeral home at 1:45 for the 2:00 p.m. service. The funeral director told us that the chapel was completely full and that many people were standing at the back of the room.

With all the family members accounted for, we were ushered into the chapel. I felt very vulnerable and raw. I didn't want to make eye contact with anyone, so I put my head down and walked to my seat. Once I was seated, I glanced around the room and saw that it was filled beyond capacity. Mom had said that she wanted all her friends at her funeral, and I was glad that her wishes had come true.

I hadn't started to cry yet, and, to my amazement, I didn't feel I needed to.

The room went silent as we waited for the service to begin. A few moments went by when I noticed that the service seemed to be taking a long time to start. I looked at my watch and saw that we were over seven minutes late. The piper had said that he might be delayed because he was playing in the Remembrance Day parade, but still, I was a bit worried.

Finally at ten minutes past the hour, the piper walked into the chapel in his Scottish kilt, playing the bagpipes. The haunting sound filled the room, but then suddenly, to my horror, the only sound being made was an awful screeching noise. The piper repeatedly tried to make the pipes play but to no avail.

The minister quickly walked over to the microphone and said, "Sorry folks, but the piper has to change the reed in the mouth piece; it seems that it is defective. He'll only be a minute."

There were a few chuckles and lots of shuffling of feet. I smiled and thought, well, this certainly broke the ice! It didn't seem as intense anymore.

After a short time, the piper was ready. He played a beautiful Scottish ballad that was well worth the wait; what a lovely sound it was.

Just as the ballad ended, Reverend Jones walked up to the podium and spoke lovingly and kindly about Mom and her life. When he was finished speaking, a soloist stood up and sang, "All My Trials Lord, Soon Be Over". Her beautiful voice rang throughout the chapel.

After the song, the minister called my husband Corky up to the podium to say a few words. Corky had wanted to share his feelings about Mom and had written a eulogy for her. He stood confidently behind the podium and unfolded his notes in preparation.

He started, "Anne was my mother-in-law. I'm sure everyone is very familiar with the stereotype that a mother-in-law is frequently saddled with. But from the very first time I met Anne until the last hours that we shared together, she always dispelled that myth. She was a loving, giving, joyful woman who consistently maintained a positive and cheerful outlook, even though she had to endure some of life's hardest lessons.

"Her goodwill, unselfishness, and generosity spilled over into the lives of the people she touched, and that made her a good mother, a good grandmother, and a good friend—especially a good friend.

"I thought of Anne more as a friend than as my mother-in-law. I think that Carole and Vern, her children, would agree that she was not only their mother, but also their friend as well. I once read somewhere that if a person during his life can count one true friend, then he should consider his life rich indeed. I believe Anne was that friend who made many people's lives richer, and when she died we all lost that one true friend. However, we will not lose the memories of the time we have known her, and for that there is joy."

Corky cleared his throat and then went on, "Anne requested that her favorite song 'Amazing Grace' be sung."

Corky walked back and sat beside me. I leaned over and whispered, "That was wonderful. Thank you."

The soloist sang 'Amazing Grace' with so much emotion that tears were streaming down her face. This song brought out powerful feelings in everyone. I glanced around and found there was hardly a dry eye in the room.

I looked down at Nigel. His little head was bent and tears were dropping onto his pants. I put my arm around him and held him close. I wondered how Tess was doing.

I was surprised at my strength. I'm sure I was the only one who was not crying in the room. I would save my tears for later, after everyone had gone.

The minister said a few more words; we said a prayer for Mom and recited the Lord's Prayer. The piper played 'Amazing Grace' to close the ceremony.

As the sound of the pipes filled the chapel, I looked up to where Mom's picture was placed on the table at the front of the room. I had to chuckle. I couldn't stop the smile that came across my face. I could not help but visualize Mom dancing in front of everyone.

There she was in a forest-green sweater, a green plaid kilt, and green knee socks, her hair tied back into a low ponytail with a green ribbon. Her big, brown eyes were shining, and she was smiling brightly. She was doing the highland sword dance, the one she used to do as a child. She was jumping high and circling round and round with her hands moving up and down. Her toes were pointing swiftly back and forth to each knee. Her body was moving perfectly to the sound of the pipes. She looked young, happy, and very much alive.

My heart swelled with gratitude. Yes, this is how I wanted to remember her. At that moment, I felt elated. All her trials *were* over. She was out there somewhere, dancing. I knew then it had all been worth it.

This was not an ending. For Mom, it was just the beginning.

Bibliography

Maggie Callahan and Patricia Kelley. *Final Gifts: Understanding the Special Awareness, Needs and Communications of the Dying.* New York, NY: Poseidon Press, 1992.

About the Author

Carole has a busy counselling practice in Vancouver and the Okanagan Valley in British Columbia, Canada. Carole has recently completed her Master's in the Vedic Sciences at UVA in Texas.

A year after her Mother's death, Carole was adamant that no one should have to die alone in a hospital, so she volunteered as one of the eight board members on the Board of Hospice in Vernon, B.C. These eight board members raised enough money to construct a beautiful non-profit hospice house. The hospice house started with six private bedrooms that has now grown to 12 bedrooms and is considered the jewel of this community. It is a place where people from all walks of life can die surrounded by loved ones in a peaceful and caring setting.

www.ingramcontent.com/pod-product-compliance
Lightning Source LLC
Chambersburg PA
CBHW030431290526
45786CB00001B/231